G000269708

ClearRevise®

Edexcel GCSE
History 1HI0

Illustrated revision and practice

Option 10:
Crime and punishment in Britain, c1000–present
and Whitechapel, c1870–c1900: crime, policing and
the inner city

Published by
PG Online Limited
The Old Coach House
35 Main Road
Tolpuddle
Dorset
DT2 7EW
United Kingdom

sales@pgonline.co.uk
www.clearrevise.com
www.pgonline.co.uk
2023

PG ONLINE

PREFACE

Absolute clarity! That's the aim.

This is everything you need to ace Paper 1 and beam with pride. Each topic is laid out in a beautifully illustrated format that is clear, approachable and as concise and simple as possible.

Each section of the specification is clearly indicated to help you cross-reference your revision. The checklist on the contents pages will help you keep track of what you have already worked through and what's left before the big day.

We have included worked exam-style questions with answers. There is also a set of exam-style questions at the end of each section for you to practise writing answers. You can check your answers against those given at the end of the book.

LEVELS OF LEARNING

Based on the degree to which you are able to truly understand a new topic, we recommend that you work in stages. Start by reading a short explanation of something, then try to recall what you've just read. This will have a limited effect if you stop there but it aids the next stage. Question everything. Write down your own summary and then complete and mark a related exam-style question. Cover up the answers if necessary but learn from them once you've seen them. Lastly, teach someone else. Explain the topic in a way that they can understand. Have a go at the different practice questions – they offer an insight into how and where marks are awarded.

Design and artwork: Jessica Webb / PG Online Ltd

First edition 2023   10 9 8 7 6 5 4 3 2 1
A catalogue entry for this book is available from the British Library
ISBN: 978-1-910523-85-8
Copyright © PG Online 2023
All rights reserved

Printed on FSC certified paper by Bell and Bain Ltd, Glasgow, UK.

THE SCIENCE OF REVISION

Illustrations and words

Research has shown that revising with words and pictures doubles the quality of responses by students.[1] This is known as 'dual-coding' because it provides two ways of fetching the information from our brain. The improvement in responses is particularly apparent in students when they are asked to apply their knowledge to different problems. Recall, application and judgement are all specifically and carefully assessed in public examination questions.

Retrieval of information

Retrieval practice encourages students to come up with answers to questions.[2] The closer the question is to one you might see in a real examination, the better. Also, the closer the environment in which a student revises is to the 'examination environment', the better. Students who had a test 2–7 days away did 30% better using retrieval practice than students who simply read, or repeatedly reread material. Students who were expected to teach the content to someone else after their revision period did better still.[3] What was found to be most interesting in other studies is that students using retrieval methods and testing for revision were also more resilient to the introduction of stress.[4]

Ebbinghaus' forgetting curve and spaced learning

Ebbinghaus' 140-year-old study examined the rate at which we forget things over time. The findings still hold true. However, the act of forgetting facts and techniques and relearning them is what cements them into the brain.[5] Spacing out revision is more effective than cramming – we know that, but students should also know that the space between revisiting material should vary depending on how far away the examination is. A cyclical approach is required. An examination 12 months away necessitates revisiting covered material about once a month. A test in 30 days should have topics revisited every 3 days – intervals of roughly a tenth of the time available.[6]

Summary

Students: the more tests and past questions you do, in an environment as close to examination conditions as possible, the better you are likely to perform on the day. If you prefer to listen to music while you revise, tunes without lyrics will be far less detrimental to your memory and retention. Silence is most effective.[5] If you choose to study with friends, choose carefully – effort is contagious.[7]

1. Mayer, R. E., & Anderson, R. B. (1991). Animations need narrations: An experimental test of dual-coding hypothesis. *Journal of Education Psychology*, (83)4, 484–490.

2. Roediger III, H. L., & Karpicke, J.D. (2006). Test-enhanced learning: Taking memory tests improves long-term retention. *Psychological Science*, 17(3), 249–255.

3. Nestojko, J., Bui, D., Kornell, N. & Bjork, E. (2014). Expecting to teach enhances learning and organisation of knowledge in free recall of text passages. *Memory and Cognition*, 42(7), 1038–1048.

4. Smith, A. M., Floerke, V. A., & Thomas, A. K. (2016) Retrieval practice protects memory against acute stress. *Science*, 354(6315), 1046–1048.

5. Perham, N., & Currie, H. (2014). Does listening to preferred music improve comprehension performance? *Applied Cognitive Psychology*, 28(2), 279–284.

6. Cepeda, N. J., Vul, E., Rohrer, D., Wixted, J. T. & Pashler, H. (2008). Spacing effects in learning a temporal ridgeline of optimal retention. *Psychological Science*, 19(11), 1095–1102.

7. Busch, B. & Watson, E. (2019), *The Science of Learning*, 1st ed. Routledge.

CONTENTS

Crime and punishment in Britain, c1000–present

Key topic 1 c1000–c1500: Crime and punishment in medieval England

Specification point ☑

Key topic 2 c1500–c1700: Crime and punishment in early modern England

Specification point ☑

Key topic 3 c1700–c1900: Crime and punishment in eighteenth- and nineteenth-century Britain

Specification point ☑

Key topic 4 c1900–present: Crime and punishment in modern Britain

Specification point ☑

Key topic 5   Whitechapel, c1870–c1900: crime, policing and the inner city

Specification point   ☑

MARK ALLOCATIONS

Green mark allocations [1] on answers to in-text questions throughout this guide help to indicate where marks are gained. A bracketed '1' e.g. [1] = one valid point worthy of a mark.

Higher mark questions require extended responses. Marks are not given as the answers should be marked as a whole in accordance with the levels on **pages 67–69**.

Understanding the specification reference tabs

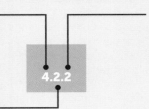

This number refers to the key topic. In this example, *Crime and punishment in modern Britain.*

This number refers to the bullet point. In this example, *The abolition of the death penalty.*

This number refers to the subtopic. In this example, *The nature of law enforcement and punishment.*

THE EXAM

Paper 1 is split into two sections: Section A and Section B. The questions follow the same format every year, so make sure you're familiar with them before the big day.

Q1   Section A — 'Describe two features of...'

This question tests your knowledge of **key features and characteristics** of the period. There are four marks available and you'll be awarded two marks for identifying two unique features, and two marks for providing supporting evidence for each unique feature.

Q2 (a)   Section A — 'How useful are Sources A and B into an enquiry about...'

This question tests your ability to **evaluate two sources** and judge how useful they are for an **enquiry** (an historical investigation). The sources will be given in the exam, and you need to think about the sources' **provenance**: **when** the sources were created, **who** created them, **why** the sources were created and **what** the sources contain. You should evaluate the **usefulness** of the sources, as well as any **limitations** that they have, for example, a written source could be one-sided, or a photograph could have been posed. This question is worth 8 marks, and you need to evaluate both the sources to get top marks.

Q2 (b)   Section A — 'How could you follow up Source A to find out more about...'

This question tests your ability to **analyse and use sources**. You will be asked to follow up one of the sources from Q2 (a). You need to suggest: a relevant detail you want to follow up, a question you want to ask, a type of source you could use to answer your question and a reason why you have chosen this type of source. Your answer booklet will provide sentence starters to help structure your answer. You will be awarded one mark for each valid point, up to a maximum of 4 marks.

Q3   Section B — 'Explain one way the ... was similar/different to...'

This question tests your ability to recognise **similarities or differences** between two historical time periods by using your **knowledge and understanding**. There are four marks available for this question. You will need to analyse features of the period to explain a similarity or difference, and support this with specific knowledge.

Q4   Section B — 'Explain why...'

This question tests your understanding of **causation** (**why** something happened). You need to use your own knowledge, but there will be two stimulus points to help you. To get top marks, you need to include information that goes beyond these stimulus points. This question is worth 12 marks, so make sure your answer includes sufficient detail.

Q5 or 6   Section B — 'How far do you agree...'

For the final question, you'll have the choice of two questions but you only need to answer one. Both questions will give a statement, and you need to say how far you agree with it. There are 16 marks available for the content of your answer, and you need to demonstrate knowledge of **continuity, change and significance**. You'll be given two stimulus points, but you also need to include your own knowledge to secure top marks. Your answer needs to reach a judgement and it must be justified with supporting evidence. There are 4 additional marks available for spelling, punctuation and grammar, so make sure you carefully re-read your answer at the end and correct any errors clearly.

TOPICS FOR PAPER 1

Option 10:
Crime and Punishment, c1000–present *and* Whitechapel, c1870–c1900

Information about Paper 1

Written exam: 1 hour 15 minutes
30% of total GCSE
52 marks (16 for Historic Environment, 36 for Thematic Study)

Specification coverage

Thematic study

Key topic 1 - c1000–c1500: Crime and punishment in medieval England

Key topic 2 - c1500–c1700: Crime and punishment in early modern England

Key topic 3 - c1700–c1900: Crime and punishment in eighteenth- and nineteenth-century Britain

Key topic 4 - c1900–present: Crime and punishment in modern Britain

Historic Environment

Key topic 5 - Whitechapel, c1870–c1900: crime, policing and the inner city

Questions

The paper is divided into two sections:

Section A Historic Environment: One question that assesses knowledge and a two-part question based on two sources.

Section B Thematic Study: Three questions that assess knowledge and understanding. There are two options for the third question.

CRIMES AGAINST THE PERSON, PROPERTY AND AUTHORITY DURING THE ANGLO-SAXON PERIOD

The Anglo-Saxons were a group of settlers who arrived from mainland Europe in the 5th century. Anglo-Saxon kings ruled parts of Britain until the Norman Conquest in 1066.

Anglo-Saxon crimes

Anglo-Saxon kings helped to establish a legal code. This legal code decreed what was a criminal offence and how these offences should be punished. Most crimes could be categorised as:

 Crimes against the person: e.g. murder, rape, assault.

 Crimes against property: e.g. theft, arson (setting fire to someone's property).

 Crimes against authority: e.g. treason (disloyalty to the king), poaching (see below).

Poaching is the act of hunting wild animals on someone else's land, and landowners viewed this as a crime against their authority. Many Anglo-Saxons considered poaching a **social crime**: something that was accepted by most members of the community. Poaching became more widespread following William I's Forest Laws (see **page 6**).

The person accused of committing a crime would be judged in the court system (see **page 4**) and then, if found guilty, would receive a punishment depending on the severity of their crime (see **page 5**).

Anglo-Saxon kings introduced the concept of the **King's Peace**, which effectively meant maintaining law and order. When it was first introduced, it specifically applied to the king, his household and individuals directly connected to the king.

ROLE OF THE AUTHORITIES AND LOCAL COMMUNITIES IN LAW ENFORCEMENT DURING THE ANGLO-SAXON PERIOD

Anglo-Saxon communities were small and close-knit: everyone knew each other. Crime rates were low, but if a crime was committed, the community worked together to bring the criminal to justice.

There was no police force in the medieval period, so local communities played an important role in maintaining law and order up and down the country.

Anglo-Saxon communities

At the start of the 11th century, England was split into earldoms. Each earldom was controlled by an earl on behalf of the king, and earls were responsible for maintaining law and order in the area they controlled. Earldoms could cover large areas, so they were split into smaller areas of land called **shires**. Shires were then broken down into **hundreds**. Each hundred comprised of ten **tithings**: a group of ten families. All men over the age of 12 in each tithing were responsible for the behaviour of the others (see below).

Shire reeves

Each shire had a **reeve** who was responsible for bringing suspects to court and making sure punishments were carried out. The title 'shire reeve' eventually became the word '**sheriff**'.

Tithings

If one member of a tithing committed a crime, the other members were responsible for bringing the criminal to justice. If the suspect evaded capture or wasn't brought to court, the whole tithing could be fined.

Tithings and the hue and cry are examples of **collective responsibility**, where people are responsible for the actions of others.

The hue and cry

When a crime was committed, the victim or any witnesses were expected to shout to alert other members of the community who would gather and search for the criminal. This was known as the **hue and cry**. If a villager didn't have a good reason for joining the hue and cry, they could be fined.

Criminals who weren't caught or refused to attend court (see **page 4**) became **outlaws**: someone who was no longer protected by society. It was illegal to assist an outlaw (i.e. by giving them food or shelter), and another person could kill an outlaw without facing criminal charges.

The court system

Once a suspect had been caught, they were put on trial. The nature of the crime and the social status of the criminal decided which court the suspect was tried at.

Royal court

The king presided over trials involving members of the nobility or very serious crimes.

Shire courts

Shire courts met at least twice a year to hear trials from their local area. Crimes such as murder were held at shire courts.

Hundred courts

Hundred courts were smaller, local courts which met once a month. They dealt with minor crimes, and justice was delivered by the reeve and a jury of local men.

The trial

Oaths

If the accused maintained their innocence, they would swear an **oath of innocence**. These oaths were sworn before God, so they were taken seriously. The accused could also call upon other people to make oaths of innocence on their behalf.

Trial by ordeal

If the jury couldn't decide if a person was guilty, they would conduct a **trial by ordeal**. The accused would endure a physical challenge, and people believed that God would influence the outcome of the trial to demonstrate a person's guilt or innocence.

Trial by ordeal is an example of how religion was involved in criminal cases. See **page 12** for more.

Trial by boiling water

The accused submerged a hand into boiling water. If the burned skin healed well, they were innocent. If it didn't, they were guilty.

Trial by hot iron

The accused held a red-hot piece of metal. If the wound was healing well several days later, the suspect was found innocent. If it wasn't, they were found guilty.

Trial by water

The accused was tied up and thrown into water. If they sank, they were innocent (and would be pulled out before they drowned). If they floated, they were guilty.

THE EMPHASIS ON DETERRENCE AND RETRIBUTION, c1000–c1066

Punishments in the Anglo-Saxon period

If found guilty, the accused was punished. The more severe the crime, the more severe the punishment. Punishments aimed to:

- stop other people from committing crimes (**deterrence**).
- punish the wrongdoer and deliver justice on behalf of those affected by the crime (**retribution**).
- protect society by executing a violent criminal (for capital offences).

Punishments were often harsh and took place in public to deter others from committing crimes.

Most severe

Murder

Punishment: **Capital punishment**. Execution by beheading or hanging and payment of a Wergild (see below).

Theft

Punishment: **Corporal punishment**. The offender might have a hand cut off.

> **Corporal** punishment means hurting or maiming someone (i.e. cutting off someone's hand). It aimed to punish the wrongdoer, but also reminded others of the consequences of breaking the law.
>
> **Capital** punishment means executing someone.

Injuring another person

Punishment: **Compensation**. The culprit had to pay a **Wergild** (a monetary fine) to the victim (or victim's family if they died). The amount paid depended on the social status of the victim. The more powerful the victim, the higher the price. The practice of Wergild aimed to prevent **blood feuds**: violent retaliation from a victim or victim's family against the perpetrator.

Disobeying someone in authority

Punishment: **Corporal punishment** or **capital punishment**. The offender might be whipped for a minor violation, but more serious offences could be viewed as acts of treason which were punishable by hanging.

Public drunkenness

Punishment: **Humiliation**. Guilty people could be locked in the **stocks** (wooden boards with holes for feet and hands) or **pillories** (wooden boards with holes for head and hands), and members of the community might shout abuse or throw things at the perpetrator. This aimed to shame the offender.

Least severe

CHANGING DEFINITIONS OF CRIME AS A RESULT OF THE NORMAN CONQUEST

In 1066, England was invaded and conquered by the Normans (people from Normandy, France). A Norman Duke, William, became the King of England.

New crimes and stricter punishments

After the conquest, Anglo-Saxons outnumbered Normans 300 to 1, and many Anglo-Saxons were unhappy that they had been conquered. Consequently, King William I introduced new laws and stricter punishments to reinforce his authority and protect his position.

Many of the Anglo-Saxon laws about crimes against people, property and authority (see **page 2**) stayed the same after the Norman conquest.

Punishment for rebellion

Between 1068–1071 there were several Anglo-Saxon uprisings against Norman rule. There was one particularly serious rebellion in the North in 1069. William responded by punishing the Anglo-Saxon nobles who were responsible for organising the rebellion, as well as local people. William's forces killed hundreds of people and destroyed their homes and crops, and many more died from starvation. This became known as the **Harrying of the North**. William's harsh punishment of the North aimed to deter other parts of the country from rebelling.

Inciting a rebellion had been a criminal offence during the Anglo-Saxon period, but the severity of the punishment towards those not directly responsible was much harsher following the Norman conquest.

Forest Laws

Approximately 30% of England became the **Royal Forest** (land that was owned by the Crown), and any Anglo-Saxons who had been living on this land were evicted. William charged people to hunt in the Royal Forests, and anyone caught poaching on Crown lands could be executed.

The effect of the Forest laws
Prior to the **Forest Laws**, many forests were considered common land (land that could be used by anyone) and people depended on these forests for their survival. Access to forests provided people with land to raise their livestock, a place to hunt for food and to gather firewood. The Forest Laws severely restricted some people's access to land.

Murdrum fine

The **murdrum law** stipulated that if a Norman was killed by an Anglo-Saxon, the people in the area where the body was found had to pay a large fine to the king.

This made it a more serious offence to kill a Norman than an Anglo-Saxon.

Changes to the definition of crimes in the later medieval period

There were several changes to crimes against authority in the later medieval period which aimed to protect landowners, the king, and the Church.

Asking for higher wages

In 1348, the Black Death swept through England. It was an epidemic of the plague which killed approximately 30% of England's population. This resulted in a shortage of labourers, and those workers who survived recognised that they were in demand. As a result, they started to ask for higher wages for their labour. In 1351, a law called the **Statute of Labourers** was introduced. This made it a crime to ask for higher pay or to move elsewhere in search of higher wages.

The Statute of Labourers is an example of how authorities can manipulate laws to benefit those with power.

Treason

The 1351 **Treason Act** extended the definition of treason. It made a distinction between **high treason** (disloyalty to the king) and **petty treason** (murdering a superior, i.e. if a servant killed his master, or a wife killed her husband). The punishment for both was execution (see **page 5**), and the guilty person's property would either revert to the Crown (in cases of high treason), or their lord (in cases of petty treason).

King William I introduced the **feudal system** to England which meant that peasants and servants were controlled by their Lord.

Heresy

Some people in the medieval period criticised the Church for amassing wealth and power, rather than focusing on the word of God and serving the local community. The Church wanted to punish those who challenged its authority, so the king and Church passed laws against **heresy** (speaking out against God or the Church) in 1382, 1401 and 1414. Convicted heretics could be executed.

ROLE OF THE AUTHORITIES AND LOCAL COMMUNITIES IN LAW ENFORCEMENT DURING THE NORMAN AND LATER MEDIEVAL PERIOD

After the conquest, much of the Anglo-Saxon law enforcement system stayed the same (see **pages 3–4**), but the Normans introduced a few changes.

Changes to law enforcement after the Norman conquest

Foresters

Foresters patrolled the Royal Forest to make sure that the Forest Laws (see **page 6**) were being followed. Those caught poaching and trespassing could be severely punished.

Trial by combat

The Normans introduced **trial by combat**, which would be used in a similar way as trial by ordeal (see **page 4**), when guilt couldn't be proven in court. The accused and their accuser would fight each other, often to the death. If the accused surrendered, they would often be executed anyway. It was believed that God influenced the outcome of the duel to indicate who was guilty and who was innocent. Trial by ordeal was abolished in 1215 (see **page 12**).

The Normans built about 500 castles between 1066–1090. These castles helped the Normans to control Britain and intimidate the Anglo-Saxon population.

Role of the Church

The Normans introduced Church courts. These courts tried crimes committed by clergymen, and **moral crimes**, such as adultery. See **page 12** for more.

Changes to law enforcement after the Norman conquest

Coroners

The role of **coroner** was introduced in 1194. Coroners were appointed to investigate and record details about suspicious deaths.

Keepers of the Peace

Keepers of the Peace were introduced around 1195. They were knights appointed to keep the King's Peace (see **page 2**), and were usually stationed in areas where there was discontent or high levels of disorder.

Parish constables

Parish constables were introduced around 1250. They were local people who helped to keep the peace and arrest suspects. They would lead the hue and cry (see **page 3**). The role was unpaid, and individuals would hold the position for a year.

Shire reeves / sheriffs

By the mid-1200s, if the community hadn't been able to catch a suspected criminal, the sheriff would try to find him.

Justices of the Peace

In 1327, the **Statute of Westminster** decreed that there should be men upholding the King's Peace in every area of the country. The role of Keeper of the Peace changed to become **Justices of the Peace** (JPs) in 1361, and the role became more widespread. JPs were usually members of the gentry looking to gain recognition in the local area. The role was unpaid. They had the power to arrest criminals.

Explain **one** way in which law enforcement in the period c1000–c1500 is different to law enforcement in the period c1900–present. [4]

In the modern period, most law enforcement is undertaken by the police force. The police are funded and controlled by the government, and officers are paid a salary and their jobs are permanent.

However, in the medieval period, there was a bigger emphasis on community law enforcement which was often voluntary and temporary. For example, parish constables were usually local volunteers who only held the position for a year.

This answer should be marked in accordance with the levels-based mark scheme on page 67.

THE EMPHASIS ON DETERRENCE AND RETRIBUTION, c1066 ONWARDS

Following the Norman Conquest, there were a few changes to Anglo-Saxon punishments.

Changes to punishments following the Norman conquest

Wergild

After the Norman conquest, the Wergild system (see **page 5**) ended, and fines were paid to the king, rather than the victim.

Capital and corporal punishment

The Normans punished crimes severely, and used capital and corporal punishments more frequently for lesser crimes, such as poaching, in order to assert their authority.

Changes to punishments in the later medieval period

Hanged, drawn and quartered

The punishment for high treason in the later medieval period (see **page 7**) was being **hanged, drawn and quartered**. This usually meant being hanged until near-death, then disembowelled, beheaded and cut into pieces.

In this period, high treason was the worst crime a person could commit, so the authorities wanted the punishment to reflect the serious nature of the crime and to deter others.

Burning at the stake

Heretics (people who committed heresy, see **page 7**) were punished by being **burned at the stake**.

'The Norman Conquest (1066) was the most significant factor affecting crimes against authority in the period c1000–c1500.'

How far do you agree? Explain your answer.

You **may** use the following in your answer:
- the Forest Laws
- murdrum law

You **must** also use information of your own.   [16 for content + 4 for SPaG = 20]

Your answer may include:

Agree:
- *Following the Norman conquest, William I wanted to assert his control and authority over the newly conquered Anglo-Saxon population, so he introduced new definitions of crime against authority so he could punish those who challenged him and other Normans.*
- *The murdrum law decreed that if a Norman was killed by an Anglo-Saxon, the people where the body was discovered had to pay a large fine. This made it a more serious offence to kill a Norman than an Anglo-Saxon and attempted to prevent Anglo-Saxons from rebelling against the Normans.*
- *William made 30% of England's forests into Royal Forests and so people needed the king's permission to hunt in the forests (the Forest Laws). Poaching was made a capital offence.*
- *William punished uprisings more severely than Anglo-Saxon kings had done before to protect his position and prevent other areas of the country from rebelling. William not only punished those responsible for the rebellion but also people who lived in the local community. This was evident during the Harrying of the North when villages were set on fire and thousands died from starvation after their crops were destroyed.*

Disagree:
- *Crimes against authority were not new, and continued from the Anglo-Saxon period.*
- *In the later medieval period, the Black Death (1348) caused a shortage of workers, and the 1351 Statute of Labourers made it a crime to ask for higher wages. This act protected the interests of landowners, who were usually people in authority.*
- *The 1351 Treason Act extended the definition of treason and clarified the difference between high treason (crimes against the monarch) and petty treason (crimes against other authority figures). This made it a more serious offence to harm someone in a position of authority.*
- *Criticisms of the Church led to several laws against heresy in 1382, 1401 and 1414, as the Church wanted to punish those speaking out against its authority.*

This answer should be marked in accordance with the levels-based mark scheme on pages 68–69.

To get top marks, you must refer to the question and make a judgement on the statement, having outlined the different sides of the argument. You also need to include information other than the bullet points from the question.

Make sure your answer to this question is in paragraphs and full sentences. Bullet points have been used in this example answer to suggest some information you could include.

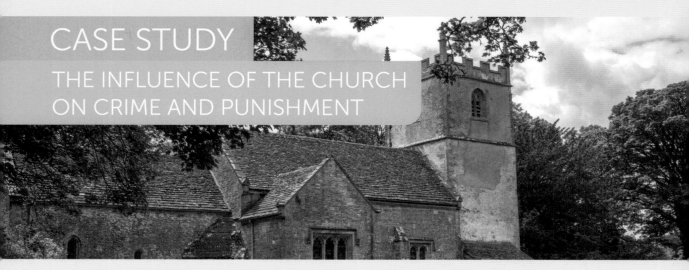

CASE STUDY
THE INFLUENCE OF THE CHURCH ON CRIME AND PUNISHMENT

The Normans introduced Church courts following the conquest in 1066.

Medieval society was very religious, so crimes against the Church and trials conducted by the Church were taken very seriously.

Crimes tried by Church courts

Church courts dealt with people accused of **religious crimes** (such as blasphemy) or **moral crimes** (such as adultery). They also tried cases where clergymen were accused of crimes (see below).

Sanctuary

Throughout the medieval period, suspected criminals could enter certain churches and claim **Sanctuary**. This meant that they couldn't be arrested because they were under the protection of the Church. The suspect usually had protection for 40 days. Within that 40-day period, they either had to agree to go to court, or if they confessed to the crime, they could swear an oath that they would leave the country.

Benefit of Clergy

Benefit of Clergy was introduced in the 12th century, and meant that any clergyman accused of a crime was tried in the Church courts. This gave the accused an advantage since the Church courts very rarely used capital punishment. In order to be tried as a clergyman, the accused had to read a specific passage from the Bible. This aimed to prove that the suspect could read, (an ability that most clergymen had, but most others didn't) and was therefore a genuine clergymen rather than an imposter hoping to get a lighter punishment.

Some criminals who were illiterate would memorise the passage and recite it to claim Benefit of Clergy with the hope of receiving a softer punishment.

Benefit of Clergy is an example of how some members of society were given preferential treatment.

Trial by ordeal

The Church was involved in trial by ordeal (see **page 4**) because it was believed that God influenced the outcome of the trial to prove a person's guilt or innocence. Clergymen were sometimes subjected to **trial by consecrated** (holy) **bread**. The accused clergyman would eat bread from Communion service. If they choked, it was a sign of guilt.

In 1215, the Pope forbade clergymen from participating in trial by ordeal, and the practice ended soon after. Trial by ordeal was replaced with legal trials and juries.

CONTINUITY AND CHANGE IN CRIMES AGAINST THE PERSON, PROPERTY AND AUTHORITY, c1500–c1700

Religion was a significant factor in crime and punishment during c1500–c1700.

Many crimes against the person, property and authority that existed in the medieval period continued in the period c1500–c1700 (also known as the **early modern period**).

Heresy and treason

At the start of the 1500s, the British population was mainly Catholic, and the head of the Catholic Church was the Pope. In 1534, King Henry VIII split from the Roman Catholic Church, and made himself Supreme Head of the Church of England, replacing the Pope as the voice of religious authority in England. This caused outrage amongst some Catholics who refused to acknowledge Henry as the leader of Catholicism in England. This meant that the monarch and religion now overlapped, and acts of heresy (speaking out against the Church) could also be viewed as acts of high treason (disloyalty to the king or queen). Both these crimes were capital offences.

Religious divisions

As well as Henry VIII's split from Rome, other religious changes occurred in England during the 16th century. **Protestantism** (an alternative form of Christianity) was spreading across the country.

The spread of Protestantism during the 1500s is known as the **Reformation**.

Between 1509–1603, English monarchs switched the country's official religion several times.

| **Henry VII** 1457–1509 Catholic | → | **Henry VIII** 1509–1547 Catholic, but split the English Church from the Catholic Church. | → | **Edward VI** 1547–1553 Protestant | → | **Mary I** 1553–1558 Catholic | → | **Elizabeth I** 1558–1603 Protestant |

Each monarch faced attempted plots to overthrow them, where the plotters wanted to replace whoever was on the throne with someone of the opposite religion.

While all the monarchs between 1457–1603 executed people for treason and heresy, Mary I became known as **Bloody Mary** for her attacks against Protestants. During her reign, hundreds of Protestants went into exile and 283 prominent Protestants were burned at the stake for heresy.

Elizabeth I recognised that religion was causing a division in England, so repealed Mary I's heresy laws and tried to introduce a **Middle Way** (religious compromises that would satisfy both Catholics and Protestants). However, in 1570 the Pope encouraged English Catholics to overthrow Elizabeth, so she began to punish Catholicism more harshly to protect her position.

NEW DEFINITIONS OF CRIME, c1500–c1700

Social and economic changes led to new definitions of crime.

Vagabondage

From the late 15th century onwards, England's population increased. This, along with food shortages, led to a rise in poverty. People who were homeless and unemployed were known as **vagabonds**, and many vagabonds turned to begging and stealing to survive. The authorities were hostile towards vagabonds because they thought they were lazy, and they worried that vagabonds could rebel against the authorities. Several laws were passed to deal with vagrancy.

A man gives money to a beggar, 1569.

| 1494 | **Vagabonds and Beggars Act** |

Vagabonds could be put in the stocks and then sent back to the place where they were born.

| 1547 | **Vagrancy Act** |

Vagrants who were able to work were branded (burnt with a hot metal rod) and sold as slaves. (This was later repealed as it was seen as too harsh.)

| 1597 | **Act for the Relief of the Poor** |

Vagabonds could be categorised as **deserving** (the very old, very young or sick) or **undeserving** (those who were physically able to work).

| 1601 | **Poor Laws** |

The deserving poor could be given aid, whereas the undeserving poor could be punished, usually by whipping.

Many vagabonds didn't have a fixed address and were itinerant (moved around frequently). This made it difficult for the authorities to enforce vagrancy laws.

Smuggling

Smuggling is the act moving something (usually goods) in or out of a country illegally. In the early modern period, smuggling was used to avoid paying high taxes on goods such as wool and alcohol. Most smuggling was done by boat at night, and since there was no police force in this period, it was difficult to catch smugglers. Smuggling was viewed by many as a **social crime** (see **page 2**). Often, many people in the local community were involved (e.g. storing and transporting smuggled goods) and ordinary people benefited from cheaper prices, so smuggling often went unreported.

Poaching

During the early modern period, an increasing amount of common land that had been accessible to everyone began to be fenced off for private use. This was known as **enclosure**. Similar to William I's Forest Laws (see **page 6**), this now meant that less common land was available for hunting, which led to an increase in poaching. Poachers could receive the death penalty.

Some local people opposed enclosure by tearing down fences.

Witchcraft

Witchcraft had been a crime in the medieval period, but accusations of witchcraft were dealt with by the Church courts, so it wasn't punishable by death. However, in early modern England, fear of witchcraft increased and laws and punishments for witchcraft became harsher.

1541

Henry VIII passed the **Witchcraft Act** which made destructive or harmful acts of witchcraft a capital offence. Helpful acts of witchcraft (such as healing illnesses or finding lost items) were not considered criminal.

The 1541, 1562 and 1603 acts allowed witchcraft to be tried in common (i.e. not Church) courts. This meant that witchcraft could now be punishable by death.

1547

The 1541 Witchcraft Act was repealed under Edward VI.

1562

Elizabeth I passed the **Act Against Conjurations, Enchantments and Witchcrafts**. This act punished minor offences with jail time and public humiliation, but major offences, such as death caused by witchcraft, became a capital offence.

1603

James I passed the **Witchcraft Act** which punished anyone who was suspected of invoking evil spirits. James I was paranoid about witchcraft, and he believed that all witchcraft was evil as it was linked to the Devil.

Increased fear and paranoia around witchcraft led to witch-hunts. See **pages 20–21** for more.

Explain **one** way in which poaching in Britain during the medieval period was similar to poaching during the period c1500–c1700. [4]

Poaching in the medieval period increased following William I's Forest Laws. These laws made some common land (which had been used by the general population) property of the Crown, and it became illegal to hunt wild animals on land that had previously been accessible to everyone.

This was similar to the period c1500–c1700, as changes in land ownership due to enclosure meant that access to common land was restricted and people were forced to poach to feed their families. In both periods, the general public viewed poaching as a social crime as it was often vital to families' survival.

This answer should be marked in accordance with the levels-based mark scheme on page 67.

THE ROLE OF THE AUTHORITIES AND LOCAL COMMUNITIES IN LAW ENFORCEMENT, c1500–c1700

The population was rising, especially in more urban areas. This meant some communities needed to adopt different systems of law enforcement.

Continuity in law enforcement

Communities in the early modern period were still expected to enforce their own law and order.

The role of the JP (see **page 9**) continued. JPs were usually wealthy landowners who enjoyed the power and influence the position gave them. They oversaw town constables and town watchmen. Parish constables (see **page 9**) still existed, and they were still expected to raise the hue and cry (see **page 3**).

Town watchmen usually patrolled the streets at night with a lantern, bell and a weapon. They were used to deter criminals and keep peace on the streets. It was a voluntary role, and every male householder was expected to take their turn, but since it was unpaid, many didn't take the role seriously.

A town watchman in 1616.

Changes to religious law and order

During the early modern period, there were concerns that some people were abusing religious privileges such as **Benefit of Clergy** and **Sanctuary**. As a result, the monarch took greater control over crime and punishment, and restricted the power of the Church justice system.

Benefit of Clergy

1488 — Henry VII decreed that non-clergymen should only be able to plead Benefit of Clergy once. If a layman (i.e. non-clergyman) wasn't able to prove that he was a member of the clergy, he would be branded on the thumb so he couldn't claim Benefit of Clergy again.

1512 — Henry VIII made certain crimes, such as murder, **unclergyable**. This meant that even if the accused was a clergyman, he had to be tried in the **secular** (i.e. non-religious) courts.

1575 — Elizabeth I changed the law again so that everyone who had committed a crime, whether they were a member of the clergy or not, was tried in a secular court. It was only after conviction that clergymen could plead Benefit of Clergy which allowed them a more lenient punishment.

Sanctuary

Henry VIII abolished most church sanctuaries and those claiming Sanctuary no longer had the option to leave the country. Sanctuary was abolished entirely by James I in 1623.

'There was little change in the nature of law enforcement in the period c1000–c1700.'

How far do you agree? Explain your answer.

You **may** use the following in your answer:

- hue and cry
- Benefit of Clergy

You **must** also use information of your own.   [16 for content + 4 for SPaG = 20]

Your answer may include:

Agree:

- *There was continuity in some aspects of law enforcement in the period c1000–c1700.*
- *Throughout this period, there was no police force, so law enforcement was often the responsibility of the community. For example, there was continuity of unpaid law enforcement roles, such as Justices of the Peace and parish constables.*
- *The hue and cry, where local people were expected to raise the alarm when a crime was committed, continued.*
- *Benefit of Clergy, where clergymen were given more lenient sentences, was fairly consistent throughout the period, although some clergymen were tried in secular courts, rather than Church courts, in the early modern period.*

Disagree:

- *There was change in the medieval period, for example, the Anglo-Saxon practice of trial by ordeal was ended in 1215 when the Pope prevented clergymen from taking part.*
- *In the period c1500–c1700, the importance of Church courts declined as the monarch became the voice of religious authority following Henry VIII's break from Rome, so the Crown had more power over crime and punishment. For example, crimes of witchcraft could be tried in secular courts rather than religious courts which meant that those accused of malicious witchcraft could receive the death penalty.*
- *Religious privileges declined, and it became harder for offenders to claim Sanctuary under Henry VIII, and then it was abolished completely under James I.*

This answer should be marked in accordance with the levels-based mark scheme on pages 68–69.

To get top marks, you must refer to the question and make a judgement on the statement, having outlined the different sides of the argument. You also need to include information other than the bullet points from the question.

Make sure your answer to this question is in paragraphs and full sentences. Bullet points have been used in this example answer to suggest some information you could include.

THE CONTINUED USE OF CORPORAL AND CAPITAL PUNISHMENT

Punishments still focused on deterrence and were often conducted in public.

Continuity in punishment

Medieval punishments continued to be used in the early modern period.

 Fines were used for minor crimes.

 Corporal punishment, such as whipping and maiming, could be used for less severe crimes, such as begging.

 Hanging was used to punish people for murder, theft and witchcraft.

 Heretics (see **page 7**) were burned at the stake.

 Beheading was used to punish nobles instead of hanging.

 Being hanged, drawn and quartered was reserved for high treason.

Transportation

The early 1600s saw the rise of a new punishment: **transportation**. This involved sending convicted criminals away from England, often to colonies in America. Upon their arrival, convicts were sentenced to years of hard labour. Once they had completed their sentence, many couldn't afford to return to England, so stayed in America.

Transportation was a harsh sentence, so authorities believed it was an effective deterrent, but it was less severe than execution, and gave convicts a chance at **rehabilitation** (another chance to become a law-abiding citizen) after they had completed their sentence.

The Bloody Code

From the late 1600s, more crimes became capital offences (crimes that could be punished by execution). Although some capital offences were severe (such as murder and treason), many weren't, for example, cutting down trees. By 1688, there were fifty crimes which could be punishable by death. This harsh legal system became known as the **Bloody Code**.

After the English Civil War ended in 1651 (see **page 21**), the monarch had less control, and Parliament became more powerful. Parliament was made up of wealthy landowners who wanted to establish laws which protected their land and property. This is why cutting down trees became a capital offence.

CASE STUDY
THE GUNPOWDER PLOT

The Gunpowder Plot was an attempt to blow up King James I and the Houses of Parliament in 1605.

The Gunpowder Plot

King James I came to the throne in 1603. Prior to James, England had been a Protestant country, and many Catholics hoped that once James became king, he would allow Catholics more freedom to practise their religion. However, James I didn't change any of the country's anti-Catholic laws.

Robert Catesby, a Catholic nobleman, recruited a group of Catholic conspirators, and they plotted to blow up the Houses of Parliament, along with King James and other prominent Protestants, on 5th November 1605 so they could put a Catholic on the throne.

An anonymous letter hinting about details of the plot found its way to Robert Cecil, King James' spymaster, and on 5th November 1605, the Houses of Parliament were raided by men loyal to the king. **Guy Fawkes** (one of the plotters) was discovered with barrels of gun powder. Fawkes was arrested and tortured until he confessed and revealed the names of the other men involved in the plot.

Guy Fawkes is caught with barrels of gunpowder beneath the Houses of Parliament.

The Gunpowder Plot is an example of terrorism. See **page 32** for more.

The aftermath

In January 1606, the conspirators were found guilty of treason. They were hanged, drawn and quartered in public (see **page 11**). Heads and body parts were displayed in Westminster and London.

 James wasn't a direct descendant from the previous monarch, Elizabeth I, so there were some questions about whether he was the legitimate king. James wanted to make an example of those accused of treason to reinforce his authority.

 King James I introduced the **Oath of Allegiance** in 1606 which required English Catholics to swear allegiance to James over the Pope.

 The public execution and display of the body parts aimed to remind people of the penalty for treason to deter others from plotting against the king.

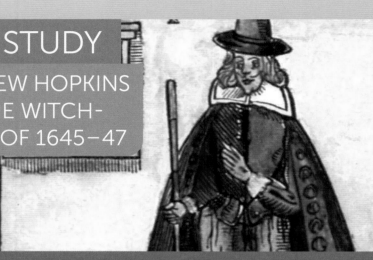

CASE STUDY
MATTHEW HOPKINS AND THE WITCH-HUNTS OF 1645–47

Matthew Hopkins (c1620–1647) was a witch hunter: someone paid to discover witches.

Witchcraft in the 17th century

Throughout the 17th century, people's fear and paranoia of witches grew. This was partly due to King James' interest in witchcraft, as he had published a book called *Daemonologie*. In the book, James discussed the existence of evil spirits, and set out the ways that witches should be punished.

The invention of the printing press in the 15th century meant that books could be produced and sold much more rapidly than before, so more people were influenced by *Daemonologie*.

Hopkins' witch-hunts

Matthew Hopkins claimed to hold the title **Witchfinder General**, and he charged local communities for his services hunting witches. He was paid for each person found guilty of being a witch. He operated mainly in Essex and East Anglia and he accused around 300 people (mainly women) of witchcraft. Of those accused, approximately 100 people were executed by hanging.

'Signs' of being a witch

 Accusations from members of the community. Often people accused another of witchcraft if they had a grudge against them or thought someone was behaving suspiciously.

 The accused had their body searched for birthmarks, boils, scars and moles. These were claimed to be the 'Devil's mark'.

 The accused would be pricked with pins, needles or blunted knives. If they didn't bleed or didn't feel pain, they could be found guilty.

 Confessions from the accused. Usually extracted under harsh treatment, such as sleep deprivation.

 Suspected witches were thrown into water, sometimes tied to a chair. If they floated, this was evidence of witchcraft.

The reasons for their intensity

Fear and paranoia surrounding witchcraft had been around for centuries, but the witch-hunts at the end of the 17th century were especially intense because:

 England experienced a Civil War between 1642–1651. The country was divided by war, and people were suspicious of each other.

 Economic problems caused by the war and poor harvests meant that people were unhappy and wanted someone to blame.

 In areas directly affected by the Civil War, authorities struggled to maintain control. Witch-hunts were a way for authorities to reassert their influence.

 With their husbands fighting in the Civil War, some women lived by themselves, and they became an easy target for accusations.

 The increased popularity of the printing press meant that books about witchcraft were more accessible. Matthew Hopkins printed his own pamphlet called *The Discovery of Witches*.

Some people opposed witch-hunts and spoke publicly against them.

Explain why there were new definitions of crimes against authority in the years c1500–c1700.

Explain your answer.

You **may** use the following in your answer:
- witchcraft
- heresy

You **must** also use information of your own. [12]

Your answer may include:
- *An increase in the population led to an increase in poverty. Consequently, there were more homeless people without employment who had to turn to begging or stealing to survive. The authorities were fearful of vagabonds because they worried that they could cause rebellions, so the Crown passed more laws to clamp down on vagabondage during the period.*
- *Between c1500–c1700 there was a greater fear of witchcraft. This was partly caused by laws created by the reigning monarchs against witchcraft, including King James I's personal attacks on witchcraft, and partly caused by the economic and social instability caused by the Civil War. There were several laws passed against harmful acts of witchcraft, and this also led to witch-hunts in the 1640s.*
- *In 1534, Henry VIII broke away from the Roman Catholic Church and he became the voice of religious authority in England. Consequently, anybody who spoke out against religion could be accused of treason as well as heresy. Both crimes carried the death penalty.*
- *Smuggling increased in the period c1500–c1700 due to the high taxes that the authorities placed on certain goods, such as wool and alcohol.*

This answer should be marked in accordance with the levels-based mark scheme on page 68.

Make sure your answer to this question is in paragraphs and full sentences. Bullet points have been used in this example answer to suggest some information you could include.

To get top marks you need to include information other than the bullet points in the question.

CONTINUITY AND CHANGE IN CRIMES AGAINST THE PERSON, PROPERTY AND AUTHORITY, c1700–c1900

Theft, poaching and smuggling continued in this period.

Highway robbery

Highway robbery emerged in the 18th century. **Highwaymen** (usually armed men on horseback) would attack a carriage or stagecoach carrying wealthy travellers on an isolated stretch of road and force them to hand over their valuables. Highway robbery increased because:

 More and better roads were built, so more people travelled. Isolated roads between towns provided an opportunity for highwaymen to strike.

 Most people carried valuables on their person because banks hadn't been established.

 Increased trade meant that more valuables were being transported between towns.

Highway robbery was a capital offence included in the Bloody Code (see **page 18**).

Highway robbery declined around the 1830s because:

- the authorities sent men to patrol highways to protect travellers and deter highwaymen.
- it became a capital offence to be armed and disguised on the road in 1772.
- travellers began using the railways instead of horse-drawn coaches for longer journeys.
- turnpikes and toll roads (where road users had to pay a fee to continue their journey) became more widespread, and it became harder for highwaymen to evade capture.

Poaching

Poaching continued in this period. Some poached out of necessity to feed their families, but some large-scale poaching gangs began to emerge during the 18th century.

The government attempted to address the problem of poaching by introducing the **Waltham Black Act** in 1723. This act criminalised carrying a weapon in a forest with a blackened face (poachers often blackened their faces to disguise themselves), and if convicted, individuals could be executed.

Smuggling

High taxes on items such as tea, wine, spirits and lace meant that smuggling boomed in the 17th and 18th centuries, and professional gangs of smugglers emerged, such as the **Hawkhurst Gang**. Authorities tried to clamp down on smuggling by patrolling the coastline, but because of the large area that officers had to cover, smugglers could often slip past unnoticed. Smuggling was still seen by many as a social crime (see **page 2**).

In 1840, the government reduced taxes on some items, which meant that smuggling became less profitable, so it declined.

CHANGING DEFINITIONS OF CRIME, c1700–c1900

The authorities put an end to witchcraft accusations, but clamped down on trade unions.

The end of witchcraft prosecutions

In 1736, a new **Witchcraft Act** was introduced. This act made it a criminal offence to claim an individual had magic powers or that they were practising witchcraft. Those convicted faced fines or imprisonment.

This Act essentially claimed that witchcraft wasn't real, and anyone alleging to have magical powers was a liar attempting to cheat gullible people out of money.

There were several reasons why people no longer believed in witchcraft.

 An increased interest in science meant that public opinion moved away from supernatural explanations for the unknown. The Royal Society was a scientific community founded in 1660 and supported by King Charles II which helped to provide scientific explanations for some supposed acts of witchcraft.

 Following the end of the Civil War in 1651, the country entered a period of political and economic stability so people were more content. People no longer needed to find others to blame.

 Prominent individuals, such as John Holt (1642–1710) who was Lord Chief Justice, were more sceptical about witchcraft. Holt acquitted several people accused of witchcraft which encouraged others to do the same.

Explain **one** way in which the accusations of witchcraft in c1500–c1700 were different to accusations of witchcraft in c1700–c1900. [4]

In c1500–c1700, the authorities believed in witchcraft and thought that the Devil gave people supernatural abilities. Consequently, witchcraft was associated with evil, so the authorities passed laws which made witchcraft a criminal offence which could be punishable by death.

In contrast, in c1700–c1900, thanks to an increased interest in scientific thinking, the authorities acknowledged that witchcraft was not real. As a result, laws were passed which made it a criminal offence to claim someone was a witch, and accusers would be expected to pay a fine or spend time in prison.

This answer should be marked in accordance with the levels-based mark scheme on page 67.

The Tolpuddle Martyrs

Trade unions are groups of people who work in a particular industry and represent the rights of those workers. Trade unions can put pressure on authorities and demand better pay and working conditions. In the 1800s, the government tried to suppress trade unions because they were fearful of the influence these groups could have.

Between 1789–1799, working-class people in France had overthrown the monarchy. There were concerns that something similar could happen in Britain.

In 1833, a group of six farm workers from the Dorset village of Tolpuddle were concerned that their wages had been reduced, so they formed a trade union to ask for guarantees that their wages wouldn't be cut any further. Other farm workers wanted to join their trade union, and prospective members were asked to swear an oath and pay a fee to join.

This guide was produced in the village of Tolpuddle.

The authorities were concerned by the growing popularity of the group and wanted to break it up, but it wasn't illegal to form a trade union, so the authorities had to find another way to stop them. Eventually, in 1834, they were able to charge the group's leaders with swearing a secret oath, which was illegal, and the group was disbanded. The leaders of the trade union were put on trial, found guilty, and given the maximum punishment for their crime: seven years of transportation to Australia. The severity of the punishment shows how desperate the authorities were to prevent others from forming trade unions.

Reaction to the sentence

The public were outraged by the sentence the men received, and they became known as the **Tolpuddle Martyrs**. A petition in favour of the martyrs received 200,000 signatures, and there were several demonstrations and protests about their treatment which drew large crowds. In 1836, the Tolpuddle Martyrs were pardoned and were permitted to return home.

The significance of the Tolpuddle Martyrs

- The government was prepared to use the law to protect their own interests and make an example of those who posed a threat.
- The public's support showed that many people believed that employees should be treated fairly by their employers.
- The government's decision to pardon the martyrs showed that they were prepared to respond to public pressure.

The Tolpuddle Martyrs

THE ROLE OF AUTHORITIES AND LOCAL COMMUNITIES IN LAW ENFORCEMENT, c1700–c1900

This period saw the introduction of modern policing.

Changes to communities

The **Industrial Revolution** (c1750–c1840) was the development of factory production in England. Most of these factories were built in urban areas, which saw a massive increase in population as people moved from the countryside to find work. As urban populations grew, so did crime rates.

 Previously, people lived in tight-knit communities where everyone knew each other. This kept crime rates low, because people didn't want to commit a crime against someone they knew personally, or because they knew it would be difficult to hide their identity. Once people moved away from close-knit communities, they became more anonymous and some became more prepared to commit crimes.

 Poverty increased in urban areas, and some had to turn to crime to survive.

 Town watchmen (see **page 16**) were supposed to deter criminals, but the position was unpaid so many didn't do their job properly or were open to bribes.

Thief-takers

One solution to the problem of increased crime were **thief-takers**: men who charged a fee for capturing criminals and returning stolen goods to victims. Some thief-takers were scammers who committed crimes, and then were paid to return valuables to their victims.

The Bow Street Runners

The **Bow Street Runners** were considered the first police force in Britain. They were founded in 1749 by brothers Henry and John Fielding. The Fielding brothers were magistrates at Bow Street Magistrates' Court in London, and they initially recruited six men, who helped to prevent and fight crime in the area.

From 1785, the Bow Street Runners were given a government grant, which was the first time that the authorities had funded law enforcement. The Bow Street Runners were effective, and had around 70 members by 1800.

The Bow Street Runners capturing a mugger.

The Bow Street Runners marked a change in law enforcement. They were a move away from unpaid, community policing towards a paid, professional organisation. However, they had a limited impact because they only operated in a small area of London, so didn't improve policing on a nationwide scale.

The development of police forces

The Bow Street Runners proved that a government-backed police force could help to reduce crime rates. Since the Bow Street Runners only operated in a small area of London, the government recognised the need for a larger police force to maintain law and order.

In 1829, Robert Peel (see **page 31**) established the **Metropolitan Police Force**, a government-funded organisation that patrolled the streets of London to deter criminals. Officers would walk the same routes every day, and these routes were known as **beats**.

The Metropolitan Police Force helped to reduce crime rates, so the government introduced the **Police Act** in 1856, which made it compulsory to establish police forces elsewhere in the country.

Between 1829–1856 areas outside of London still used parish constables.

The beginning of the CID

Initially, the Metropolitan Police Force focused on preventing, rather than investigating, crimes. When it became clear that there was a need for criminal investigations, a detective branch was established 1842. This developed into the **Criminal Investigation Department** (**CID**) in 1878. Investigative police work in this period largely relied on gathering evidence and interviewing witnesses, as forensic science technology (see **page 37**) was not yet available.

Explain why there were changes to law enforcement in the period c1700–c1900.

You **may** use the following in your answer:
- The Bow Street Runners
- Metropolitan Police Force

You **must** also use information of your own.   [12]

Your answer may include:

- *The Industrial Revolution led to larger urban populations. This increased crime rates because people had moved away from their tight-knit local communities to larger, more anonymous urban populations, making it easier to commit crimes.*

- *Higher crime rates created a need for better-organised law enforcement, and the Fielding brothers established the Bow Street Runners to try to tackle crime in parts of London.*

- *Thanks to the success of the Bow Street Runners, and the work of individuals such as Robert Peel, the authorities recognised that a government-funded police force would help to address crime in the wider London area.*

- *The success if the Metropolitan police force, led to the 1856 Police Act which established police forces outside of the capital.*

- *Initially, police forces focused on preventing crimes by walking the beat. However, it became clear that a separate arm of the police force was needed to investigate crimes, so the CID was developed in 1878.*

This answer should be marked in accordance with the levels-based mark scheme on page 68.

Make sure your answer to this question is in paragraphs and full sentences. Bullet points have been used in this example answer to suggest some information you could include.

CHANGING VIEWS ON THE PURPOSE OF PUNISHMENT, c1700–c1900

The period c1700–c1900 saw increased interest in the reform and rehabilitation of convicted criminals.

The use and end of transportation

Transportation had been used as a punishment since the early 1600s (see **page 18**). Initially, criminals were sent to America, but after the American War of Independence (1776), America no longer accepted British criminals. From the 1780s, criminals were sent to Australia instead, with approximately 160,000 sent between 1787–1868. Criminals were expected to work for free for seven years. After seven years, convicts were free to leave, but many couldn't afford their passage home, so stayed. Transportation to Australia began to decline from 1840s because:

 The British prison system started to develop and more prisons were built. Criminals were sentenced to time behind bars instead of transportation.

 Gold was discovered in Australia, and many people emigrated there with the hope of finding their fortune. Australia was now attractive to non-criminals.

 People disagreed over the effectiveness of transportation. Some felt it wasn't enough of a deterrent, while others believed it was too harsh.

Public executions

Most executions took place in public as it was believed that they would act as a deterrent. However, public executions became a form of entertainment, and they drew large crowds.

Sometimes the person who was executed was cheered as a hero.

These crowds would sometimes cause more crime. Fights could break out and crowds attracted pickpockets. Concerned by the public's perception, authorities began conducting executions in private instead (usually inside a prison) and the last public execution was held in 1868.

The Bloody Code

By 1810, the number of crimes that could be punished by execution reached 222. Despite the increase in capital offences, the crime rate wasn't dropping. Some juries didn't want to sentence a petty criminal to death for a minor offence, so some crimes tended to go unpunished which encouraged other criminals. It was clear that the death penalty wasn't an effective deterrent.

Robert Peel (see **page 31**) reduced the number of crimes punishable by the death penalty in the 1820s, and this effectively ended the Bloody Code (see **page 18**).

Prison reform

Prior to the late 1700s, prisons were mainly used to hold individuals who were awaiting trial or sentencing. Prisons became commonly used for punishment from the late 1700s, following the end of transportation and the decline of the Bloody Code.

Imprisonment was often used to punish those who had debts, and inmates could stay in debtors' prisons until their debts were paid off.

Prisons were often poorly managed and the conditions were unpleasant, but some people argued that criminals didn't deserve any better.

Prison conditions

 Prisons were cramped and inmates weren't separated based on their crimes, so violent criminals could share a cell with a pickpocket.

 Sanitation was poor, so disease could spread quickly.

 Inmates were expected to pay for food, or pay to be released. Poorer prisoners often couldn't afford these fees.

Explain **one** way in which the nature of punishment in the years c1500–1700 was different from the nature of punishment c1700–c1900. [4]

In c1500–c1700, punishments were often extreme compared to the nature of the crime, for example, chopping down wood was part of the Bloody Code, so could be punishable by execution. Punishments were harsh to act as a deterrent to prevent others from committing a crime.

By the period c1700–c1900, punishments were less severe, and the number of capital offences were reduced, which ended the Bloody Code. More people believed that punishments should help to reform and rehabilitate offenders.

This answer should be marked in accordance with the levels-based mark scheme on page 67.

John Howard

John Howard (1726–1790) conducted inspections of prisons across the country and was appalled by what he found. He brought the matter before the government, and convinced them to pass two acts in 1774 to improve conditions in gaols. He recommended abolishing fees that prisoners had to pay to jailers, and suggested improvements to healthcare and sanitation.

Elizabeth Fry

Elizabeth Fry (1780–1845) was a prison reformer. She visited Newgate prison in 1813 and was horrified by the conditions that female prisoners experienced. Women were kept in the same prisons as men, which made them vulnerable to sexual abuse, so she persuaded Robert Peel (see **page 31**) to separate male and female prisoners in his 1823 Gaols Act. Fry encouraged female prisoners to learn skills such as needlework so that they could find employment once released. Fry's belief in rehabilitation inspired other prisons to adopt similar practices.

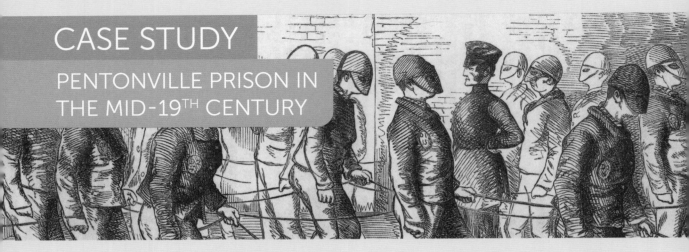

CASE STUDY

PENTONVILLE PRISON IN THE MID-19TH CENTURY

Pentonville Prison was opened in 1842. It could house 520 inmates and aimed to be a model prison which focused on reform and rehabilitation.

Reasons for its construction

Pentonville Prison was built in London following the 1839 **Prison Act** which supported the use of the **separate system**. The separate system ensured that inmates had little to no interaction with each other. This was supposed to encourage prisoners to reflect on, and feel remorse for, their crimes, and the boredom and loneliness was an additional punishment. Inmates were allowed to speak with the prison chaplain, as access to religion was believed to help reform inmates.

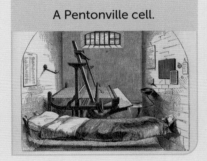

A Pentonville cell.

Features of Pentonville Prison

Each inmate had their own small cell with a hammock and bedding, a sink, a toilet and a loom (a weaving machine). The walls were thick so inmates couldn't hear each other.

Inmates were allowed to leave their cell to exercise, but they had to wear masks to stop them from talking to each other. Prisoners were allowed to attend church services, however, they sat in cubicles with high walls which meant they could only see the chaplain and not any of the other inmates.

The strengths and weaknesses of the separate system

Strengths
- ➕ Pentonville was cleaner and better run than previous prisons.

Weaknesses
- ➖ Inmates were not given an education which could improve their lives outside of prison.
- ➖ The isolation contributed to poor mental health, and suicide was not uncommon.

The impact of Pentonville

Over 50 prisons were built in the same style as Pentonville. However, crime rates weren't significantly impacted by these new prisons, and some argued that prisons like Pentonville weren't enough of a deterrent. A new Prisons Act was introduced in 1865. This instructed that life in prisons should become harsher. It encouraged the **silent system** where inmates were forced to endure hard labour, such as turning treadmills, in silence.

CASE STUDY
ROBERT PEEL

Robert Peel (1788–1850) had an enormous impact on prison reform and policing in Britain.

Prison reform

In 1822, Robert Peel became Home Secretary (a government position responsible for law and order). In 1823, Peel abolished the death penalty for over 100 crimes. He also supported the work of Elizabeth Fry (see **page 29**), and believed in the benefits of reforming the prison system. In 1823, he passed the **Gaols Act**, which introduced some improvements:

 Male and female inmates were separated, and female wardens supervised female prisoners.

 Prison staff were paid by the prison, rather than inmates.

 Regular visits from chaplains encouraged spiritual reform.

 Inmates no longer wore chains.

In reality, it took a while for Peel's reforms to be introduced because prison inspections weren't compulsory until 1853.

The development of the Metropolitan Police Force

Peel believed that policing across London should be unified and standardised. In 1829, he founded the Metropolitan Police Force to prevent crime.

There had been an economic recession in 1825–1826, which led to high unemployment rates and an increase in crime. This helped Peel push the 1829 Metropolitan Police Act through Parliament, as the government were keen to tackle crime rates.

The police force was unpopular at first. Some people were worried it would be too expensive, restrict people's freedoms, and that recruits would be poorly trained. Peel established a code of conduct, which helped to address people's concerns:

- police officers should be completely impartial, and treat everyone equally.
- officers should only use force when necessary, and were only armed with a baton.
- officers should wear a uniform that made them easily identifiable and made them look different to soldiers.
- the role was paid, and officers were provided with some training.

Police officers were given the nicknames 'bobbies' and 'peelers' after Robert Peel.

CONTINUITY AND CHANGE IN THE NATURE OF CRIMES AGAINST THE PERSON, PROPERTY AND AUTHORITY, c1900–PRESENT

Technology has changed the way that some crimes are committed.

New forms of theft

 Car theft has risen since c1900. Thieves can steal cars, re-paint them, change their number plates and re-sell them.

 The increase of technology means that digital piracy (illegally downloading or streaming music and films etc) has risen. Digital piracy is often seen as a social crime.

 Credit cards allow thieves to keep stealing from a victim until the card is blocked or the account is protected.

 Crimes such as identity theft and fraud now happen more frequently online. These crimes are often committed anonymously and remotely (sometimes from overseas), so it can be more difficult to bring the criminal to justice.

Terrorism

Terrorism can be defined as political or religious groups deliberately killing civilians to try to force world leaders to recognise and agree to the terrorist group's aims. Terrorism has existed for centuries, but it has grown during the last 200 years. Terrorists now have access to more sophisticated weapons and communication networks. Those accused of terrorism offences could face life imprisonment.
Recent examples of terrorism in the UK include:

- attacks conducted by the **IRA** (Irish Republican Army) from the 1970s to 1990s, including a car bomb in Omagh in 1998 which killed 29 people.
- the 2005 terror attacks in London conducted by Islamic terrorists where bombs were detonated on the London Underground and a bus.

The Anti-Terrorist squad was set up in 1971 to deal with terrorist threats.

Site of the Omagh bombing, 1998.

Smuggling

Smuggling still occurs, but some of the items being smuggled and how they are transported have changed.

Alcohol and cigarettes are commonly smuggled into the country to avoid import duties.

Drug smuggling

Most recreational drugs are illegal in the UK, so they are smuggled into the country via boat, plane, rail and road networks. The police use sniffer dogs, x-rays and thermal scanners to search for drugs. The penalty for drug smuggling is a fine or jail time.

People smuggling

Some people from overseas want to enter the UK illegally, often to escape violence in their own country. These immigrants will pay people smugglers to bring them across borders illegally. People smugglers face jail time if caught.

Human trafficking

Some people are brought into the UK against their will or by deception. Victims of trafficking are often forced into prostitution or slavery. Traffickers can be punished with time in prison.

In earlier periods, smuggling was seen as a social crime. However, nowadays, the general public are much less tolerant of those who smuggle people or illegal drugs.

A sniffer dog at an airport checks luggage for illegal drugs.

Explain **one** way in which smuggling in the years c1500–c1700 was different to smuggling in the years c1900–present. [4]

In the period c1500–1700, smugglers brought items such as tea, alcohol and lace into the country in order to avoid the high taxes that the government charged on these items. Since local communities were either involved in the smuggling or benefited from cheaper prices, many saw it as a social crime and didn't report it to the authorities.

However, in the period c1900–present, drugs and people are smuggled into the country because they cannot be brought into the country legally. Local communities are much less tolerant of people smuggling and human trafficking, so it is no longer viewed as a social crime.

This answer should be marked in accordance with the levels-based mark scheme on page 67.

CHANGING DEFINITIONS OF CRIME, c1900–PRESENT

Society has changed over the past 200 years, and the law has changed with it.

Decriminalisation

Some acts have been decriminalised (made legal).

July 1967

Homosexual acts between men aged 21 or older were decriminalised.

Today, the law can prosecute crimes as **hate crimes** if an offence has been committed on the basis of someone's race, religion, disability, sexual orientation or transgender identity. Hate crimes can be punished more severely.

October 1967

Abortion was made legal in certain situations, for example, if continuing the pregnancy would risk the life of the mother.

Decriminalising homosexual acts and abortion occurred because members of the public put pressure on the authorities to change the law.

Race crimes

The **Race Relations Acts** of 1965, 1968 and 1976 made it a criminal offence to discriminate someone on the grounds of colour, race or ethnic origins.

In 1976, the **Commission for Racial Equality** was established to promote racial equality, and more recently the 2006 **Racial and Religious Hatred Act** criminalised any attempts to provoke hatred based on a person's race or religion.

When the 1965 Race Relations act was introduced, there was a growing community of nearly one million immigrants living in the UK who had moved to the UK from Commonwealth countries such as India, Pakistan and Jamaica. These immigrants were often unfairly discriminated against.

Driving offences

From the middle of the 1900s, cars have become more widespread, and this has led to new driving laws which aim to make roads safer.

Drink driving has been illegal since 1872 (when it was a crime to drive a horse-drawn vehicle while drunk), but up until the 1970s, drink driving was viewed by many as a social crime. Government campaigns and new laws have attempted to change people's attitudes towards drink driving, as well as speeding and not wearing seatbelts. In 2003, it became illegal to use a mobile phone while driving.

Drug crimes

Since the 1960s, the use of drugs has been on the rise. In 1971, the government passed the **Misuse of Drugs Act** which made it illegal to possess, sell or produce drugs. The act also categorised drugs into three categories: class A, B and C. Class A drugs (such as heroin) are considered the most harmful, and offences involving these drugs are punished the most severely.

Recreational drug use is viewed by some as a social crime, so this can make it difficult for the authorities to crack down on drug-related crimes.

Some drug users may commit other crimes, such as theft, to support their habit.

'There has been little change in the nature of criminal activity in the period c1700–present.'

How far do you agree? Explain your answer.

You **may** use the following in your answer:
- smuggling
- theft

You **must** also use information of your own.   [16 for content + 4 for SPaG = 20]

Your answer may include:

Agree:
- *Smuggling has occurred throughout the period, although the goods being smuggled varied. For example, alcohol, tea and lace in c1700–c1900, and drugs and people in c1900–present.*
- *Theft happened throughout the period, however the way that theft occurs has changed. For example, in c1700–c1900, a thief would steal valuables from a victim or a victim's home. Due the rise in technology, theft can now happen online, so a thief can steal items remotely.*

Disagree:
- *Poaching happened more frequently in c1700–c1900, and laws were passed, such as the Waltham Black Act 1723, which made being in a forest with a weapon and a blackened face a capital offence. Poaching happens much less frequently in the modern period.*
- *The rise in the use of cars has led to new offences in c1900–present. For example, it is illegal to go over the speed limit or to drive while using a mobile phone.*
- *The ease of travel has increased immigration, which has led to a rise in race-related crimes. It is now illegal to discriminate someone based on their race, skin colour or religion.*
- *The rise in the availability and use of drugs has led to laws which have criminalised the possession, sale and manufacture of illegal drugs.*

This answer should be marked in accordance with the levels-based mark scheme on pages 68–69.

To get top marks, you must refer to the question and make a judgement on the statement, having outlined the different sides of the argument. You also need to include information other than the bullet points from the question.

Make sure your answer to this question is in paragraphs and full sentences. Bullet points have been used in this example answer to suggest some information you could include.

THE ROLE OF AUTHORITIES AND LOCAL COMMUNITIES IN LAW ENFORCEMENT, c1900–PRESENT

Communities still play a role in law enforcement, but the police have a responsibility for keeping people safe.

Neighbourhood Watch

Neighbourhood Watch groups were introduced in 1982 to encourage greater individual responsibility for tackling crime. Groups of residents work closely with local police officers to try to prevent and detect crime in their area. Members are not expected to apprehend criminals, instead they pass on information to the police to help keep their local area safe. The Neighbourhood Watch scheme has attracted criticisms, since many of the neighbourhoods which take part in the scheme are in wealthy, suburban areas which tend to have low crime rates.

Those communities that aren't part of a Neighbourhood Watch scheme are still encouraged to report crimes or suspicious behaviour to police via **tip lines**.

Increasing specialisation

Specialised police units have developed, and officers are given training and equipment to help them tackle specific types of crime. For example, the National Crime Agency (NCA) focuses on organised crime, such as gangs, drug rings and people trafficking, whereas the Police Central e-crime unit helps to prevent and solve cases relating to cybercrimes.

The move towards prevention

Traditionally, police officers walked the beat, but changes to policing mean that many officers are now deployed to crime scenes, or spend more time doing desk work, making them less visible to the general public.

To address this, **Police Community Support Officers** (PCSOs) were introduced in 2002. PCSOs don't have the same level of authority as police officers, but they patrol certain areas and act as a visible deterrent to criminals. Their presence can offer reassurance to law-abiding citizens.

Police Community Support Officers on the beat.

Use of science and technology

Science and technology have developed rapidly in the period c1900–present, and new techniques and equipment have been adopted by the police in the fight against crime.

The process of using scientific techniques (such as fingerprinting and analysing DNA) to help investigate crimes is known as **forensic science**.

1901 Scotland Yard began fingerprinting individuals and identifying criminals using fingerprints left at crime scenes.

1930s The Metropolitan Police introduced dogs to support beat officers.

1930s Radios installed in police cars improved communication between local officers. The '999' emergency number was introduced.

1960s Police officers were equipped with personal radios, allowing them to communicate while patrolling on foot.

1961 Video surveillance was installed at a London train station. Since then, CCTV has been widely installed and there are over 7 million CCTV cameras in the UK today.

1974 The Police National Computer (PNC) went live. This is a database accessible to law enforcement organisations across the UK which allows them to search and share information.

1980s Police forces began using DNA evidence from hair, blood etc to identify criminals.

Improvements in transport such as cars, helicopters and planes have allowed police officers to attend crime scenes or track down criminals more quickly.

Explain **one** way in which the role of local communities in law enforcement in c1500–c1700 is similar to the role of local communities in law enforcement in c1900–present. [4]

In both periods, local communities were involved in alerting law enforcement to crimes to help bring criminals to justice. In the period c1500–c1700, local people were expected to join the hue and cry when a crime had been committed to raise the alarm and to help find the perpetrator.

In the period c1900–present, local communities have formed Neighbourhood Watch schemes that pass on reports of suspicious activity to local law enforcement. In both periods, there is an emphasis on collective responsibility to try to tackle crime.

This answer should be marked in accordance with the levels-based mark scheme on page 67.

THE ABOLITION OF THE DEATH PENALTY

In the early 20th century, there were growing calls to abolish capital punishment.

Abolition of the death penalty

In the early 20th century, the public were largely in favour of the death penalty, but an increasing number of people felt it should be abolished. Because the majority of the public agreed with capital punishment, many politicians also supported it, to remain popular with voters.

Reasons for the death penalty

➕ Some argued that execution was the most effective deterrent for the most severe crimes.

➕ Some believed that execution was the only way that a victim's family could get justice for the loss of a loved one.

➕ Execution was the only way to ensure that a murderer would never kill again.

➕ Execution was cheaper than imprisonment.

Reasons against the death penalty

➖ Despite being a capital offence, people still continued to commit murder. In places where the death penalty had been abolished, incidences of murder didn't dramatically increase.

➖ Others believed that execution was not the answer and that society should be more forgiving and punish offenders with non-violent sentences, such as imprisonment.

➖ There were some cases where it was later found that an individual had been wrongfully convicted of murder (see Timothy Evans below).

Prominent death penalty cases in the 1950s encouraged some to reconsider capital punishment:

Timothy Evans (1950)

Timothy Evans was found guilty of murdering his wife and child and was hanged. Later, it was discovered that the victims were killed by the Evans' neighbour.

Derek Bentley (1953)

Derek Bentley was found guilty of murdering a police officer, despite not being the one to fire the gun. Bentley was hanged in 1953. (See **page 42**.)

Ruth Ellis (1955)

Ruth Ellis killed her abusive partner in 1955, and was hanged for her crime. The public sympathised with Ruth because of the abuse she had suffered at the hands of her boyfriend.

The end of the death penalty

1957 — The Government introduced the **Homicide Act** which reserved the death penalty for only the most severe murder cases.
1965 — The Murder (Abolition of Death Penalty) Act suspended executions in the UK.
1969 — Murder was no longer punishable by the death penalty but the death penalty still existed for certain crimes, such as treason and espionage (spying).
1999 — The death penalty was abolished entirely for all crimes.

Ruth Ellis was the last woman to be executed in the UK, and the last men to be hanged in England were executed in 1964.

CHANGES TO PRISONS

Prisons are now tailored to the types of inmates they house. Prisons are more concerned with the physical and mental well-being of inmates, and more emphasis is placed on reforming and rehabilitating offenders.

Changes to prisons

1907 The **probation** system was introduced. This is where prisoners are released from prison but they must meet with a probation officer and comply with certain rules (for example avoiding certain people and places). If they break these rules, the offender can be sent back to prison.

1920s The **separate system** (see **page 30**) ended.

1930s **Open prisons** were introduced. These prisons allow prisoners to leave during the day to go to work, and inmates can move about the prison with more freedom. Open prisons house low-risk inmates and focus on rehabilitation and reintegration into society.

1940s Whipping prisoners and the use of hard labour as punishment in prisons was abolished.

Today Inmates can apply for student loans which allow them to pursue university courses. Other inmates can learn practical skills to help them find employment once they are released.

Not everyone agrees with how the prison system is run:

- Some believe that prisoners have better access to healthcare, facilities and opportunities than the public.
- Some criticise prisons for being 'too soft'.
- The prison population is rising, suggesting that prison doesn't deter criminals.

> Today, more people agree that crime has links to poor education and drug use, so prisons try to help inmates address these issues to prevent them from reoffending.

Alternatives to prison

Some lesser crimes are given **non-custodial** (i.e. non-prison) sentences. This helps keep prison populations down, and gives petty criminals a chance at rehabilitation.

Electronic monitoring

Offenders are required to wear a tag on their ankle which can either monitor a curfew, a person's location or their alcohol consumption. Anyone found breaking their conditions of release can be sent to prison.

Community service

If convicted of minor crimes, first-time offenders or people with certain mental health conditions might be ordered to do unpaid work which benefits the community, such as removing graffiti.

Criminal Behaviour Orders

CBOs aim to address anti-social behaviour such as vandalism. A court order gives the offender rules to follow (such as avoiding certain people or places). If CBOs aren't followed, the offender might have to pay a fine or be sent to prison.

During the 20th century, authorities recognised that young offenders should be treated differently to adult offenders.

1900s   **Juvenile courts** (which try children separately from adults) and **borstals** (prisons for young offenders) and were established. Authorities were concerned that if young offenders mixed with adult prisoners they could learn how to commit more serious crimes.

1933   The age of criminal responsibility was raised from 7 to 8.

1948   The **Criminal Justice Act** stipulated that offenders under the age of 17 should not be sent to adult prisons. Youth offenders over the age of 12 should report to **attendance centres**.

1963   The age of criminal responsibility was raised from 8 to 10 in England and Wales.

1982   **Criminal Justice Act** abolished borstals and replaced them with **youth custody centres**.

1988   The first **Young Offender Institution** was opened, for offenders aged between 15–18. Inmates were expected to take part in 25 hours of education per week to prepare them to find employment after their release.

Explain why there were changes to the prison system in the period c1700 to the present day.

You **may** use the following in your answer:
- Elizabeth Fry
- open prisons

You **must** also use information of your own.   [12]

Your answer may include:

- *In the 1700s, prison conditions were poor. Cells were cramped, there was little sanitation, and male and female inmates were housed together.*

- *Reformers, such as Elizabeth Fry and John Howard, believed that prison conditions should be improved, and that they should also focus on reform and rehabilitation. Their work influenced politicians, such as Robert Peel, who introduced positive changes in his 1823 Gaols Act.*

- *Alternative forms of punishment, such as transportation and the Bloody Code, began to decline in the mid-1800s, so criminals were sentenced to prison time instead. This led to more prisons being built and a greater focus on the prison system.*

- *The 1839 Prison Act encouraged the use of the separate system and influenced the design of Pentonville prison. However, the separate system worsened the mental health of inmates, and ended in the 1920s.*

- *The 1900s led to more significant changes to the prison system with an emphasis on prisoners' reform and rehabilitation. The open system was introduced in the 1930s, which gave low-risk prisoners more freedom and allowed them to leave prison daily to go to work.*

- *Recently, prison populations have been rising, so authorities have introduced some alternatives to prison sentences, such as electronic monitoring, to prevent overcrowding.*

This answer should be marked in accordance with the levels-based mark scheme on page 68.

CASE STUDY

CONSCIENTIOUS OBJECTORS IN THE FIRST AND SECOND WORLD WARS

A Conscientious Objector is someone who refuses to fight in a war.

First World War

During the First World War (1914–1918), the 1916 **Military Service Act** made **conscription** compulsory. This meant that all physically fit, single men aged between 18–41 had to serve in the army.

There was a clause in the act which allowed men to refuse to serve if they were **Conscientious Objectors**: their moral or religious beliefs prevented them from fighting. Approximately 16,000 men refused to fight during the First World War.

COs had to attend a tribunal to decide if they should be exempt from enlisting. Only 400 men were granted total exemption, the rest became either **alternativists** or **absolutists**.

Approximately 10,000 became alternativists: people who agreed to take on non-combat roles to help the war effort. The **Non-Combatant Corps** (NCC) was formed in 1916.

Absolutists, who refused to take part in any war-related role, were sent to prison. While imprisoned, they were treated poorly to deter others from refusing to help the war effort.

COs were treated harshly in the media and by the public. Many saw COs' unwillingness to fight as cowardice. **The Order of the White Feather** encouraged women to give white feathers (a symbol of cowardice) to men of fighting age not in military uniform. This aimed to shame men into enlisting.

A postcard from the First World War mocking COs.

THE CONSCIENTIOUS OBJECTOR AT THE FRONT!

OH, YOU NAUGHTY UNKIND GERMAN — REALLY, IF YOU DON'T DESIST I'LL FORGET I'VE GOT A CONSCIENCE, AND I'LL SMACK YOU ON THE WRIST!

Several absolutists died in prison, and many suffered depression.

Second World War

Compulsory conscription was introduced again during the Second World War (1939–1945) for both men and women. Again, there was a clause which allowed people to refuse military service on the basis of their moral, ethical or religious beliefs. Approximately 59,000 refused to fight, and these people attended tribunals. Those not given exemption were either given non-combat roles or sent to prison, although far fewer were imprisoned, and the treatment they received was much less harsh.

COs were still shamed by the public and the media during the Second World War, but to a lesser extent. Many families had lost loved ones during the First World War, and soldiers who had returned were often mentally or physically wounded, so there was more sympathy for those who chose not to fight.

CASE STUDY
DEREK BENTLEY

Derek Bentley was executed in 1953 as an accomplice to murder.

The murder

On 2nd November 1952, Derek Bentley, 19, and his 16-year-old accomplice, Christopher Craig, were in the process of robbing a warehouse near London. The police interrupted the burglary, and cornered Bentley and Craig. A police officer, Frederick Fairfax, asked Craig to hand over his gun, and it's reported that Bentley said: "Let him have it, Chris."

Craig opened fire on the police officers, and Craig fatally shot Police Constable Sidney Miles.

The words spoken by Bentley were used by both the Prosecution and Defence in his subsequent trial.

The Prosecution claimed Bentley meant, "Shoot him, Chris" whereas the Defence claimed he meant "Give him the gun, Chris".

The trial

Bentley and Craig were both put on trial for murder, which was a capital offence. However, since Craig was under 18, he wasn't eligible for the death penalty. Bentley was found guilty of murder and sentenced to hang. The Home Secretary, David Maxwell Fyfe, could have asked the Queen to consider the royal prerogative of mercy (which would have allowed the Queen to pardon Bentley), but he decided against it.

Derek Bentley

Some believed Bentley shouldn't be sentenced to death for several reasons:
- Bentley did not fire the shots that killed Sidney Miles.
- Bentley had learning difficulties. He had a very low IQ and was illiterate.

There was a lot of public and political pressure to change Bentley's sentence to life in prison, rather than execution, including a letter signed by 200 MPs, public protests and media coverage. However, Bentley was hanged on 28th January 1953.

The significance of the case

Derek Bentley's death (along with several other high-profile executions) led people to put pressure on the government to abolish the death penalty (see **page 38**).

When Bentley stood trial, the English court system did not recognise the concept of **diminished responsibility**, i.e. suffering from a mental or medical condition which may have impacted a person's ability to make a rational judgement or exercise self-control. The concept of diminished responsibility was introduced into the English justice system in 1957.

EXAMINATION PRACTICE

1. Explain **one** way in which attitudes towards the death penalty in c1500–c1700 were different to attitudes towards the death penalty in c1900–present.   [4]

2. Explain why there were changes to the crime of witchcraft in the period c1000–c1750.

    You **may** use the following in your answer:
    - King James I
    - Matthew Hopkins

    You **must** also use information of your own.   [12]

3. 'The main purpose of punishment in the years c1500–c1900 was to deter people from committing crimes.'

    How far do you agree? Explain your answer.

    You **may** use the following in your answer:
    - the Bloody Code
    - Pentonville prison

    You **must** also use information of your own.   [16 for content + 4 for SPaG = 20]

4. 'Forensic science has been the most significant development in the nature of police work since the creation of the Metropolitan Police Force (1829).'

    How far do you agree? Explain your answer.

    You **may** use the following in your answer:
    - DNA
    - radios

    You **must** also use information of your own.   [16 for content + 4 for SPaG = 20]

THE CONTEXT OF WHITECHAPEL

The first part of Paper 1 will focus on Whitechapel between 1870–1900.

Problems of housing in Whitechapel

Whitechapel is an area in the east of London. In the 1800s, it was overcrowded, dirty and unsafe. One street in Whitechapel was described as 'the foulest and most dangerous' street in London.

Rookeries

Some of London's poorest residents lived in Whitechapel in slums known as **rookeries**. Records show that in 1877, one rookery had 123 rooms which housed 757 people: six people lived in each room. As well as being overcrowded, rookeries were poorly ventilated, and there were no sewers so waste ran into the streets and disease spread quickly.

Lodging houses and pubs

Those who couldn't afford to rent a room permanently or needed temporary accommodation slept in **lodging houses** or **pubs**. There were approximately 200 lodging houses in Whitechapel. Lodging houses provided cheap accommodation, but the conditions were no better than rookeries.

Some lodging houses only allowed patrons access to a bed for 8 hours. Once their time was up, someone else could rent it. This meant landlords could maximise profits by renting the same bed multiple times a day. For more on lodging houses, see **page 45**.

A London lodging house in 1870.

Some people in Whitechapel slept rough. If they had some money or the weather was particularly bad, they might rent a bed in a lodging house.

Workhouses

Workhouses offered food and shelter to those who couldn't afford to rent somewhere. In return, inmates were expected to work hard to earn their keep. Life in the workhouse was strict and unpleasant to deter only the very desperate from staying. Families were split up, food consisted of gruel (a thin porridge), bread and cheese, and the work was tough and repetitive. The workhouse in Whitechapel was South Grove. It was built in 1872, and housed up to 800 people.

Most workhouse residents consisted of the elderly, single mothers, orphans and the very sick.

Describe **two** features of life in the Whitechapel rookeries. [4]

Rookeries were overcrowded.[1] Multiple people could share one small room.[1]

Rookeries were unhygienic.[1] There was little ventilation and no sewers so disease spread quickly in rookeries.[1]

Attempts to improve housing

In 1875, the **Artisans' and Labourers' Dwellings Improvement Act** allowed the government to buy areas of slum housing, tear them down and rebuild better accommodation. An American, **George Peabody**, funded the construction of the **Peabody Estate** in Whitechapel. The estate opened in 1881, and consisted of 286 flats across 11 blocks, and the flats ranged in size from one to three rooms, with weekly rents between 3 to 6 shillings depending on the size of the flat.

Although the accommodation in the Peabody Estate was an improvement, it did not fix housing issues in Whitechapel:

 The rents were reasonable, but they were still higher than most could afford.

 The 286 flats weren't enough to re-house everyone in Whitechapel.

 People who had lived in the slums that had been torn down needed somewhere else to live. This increased overcrowding in areas around the Peabody Estate.

Poverty, unemployment and crime

Poverty and unemployment led to high rates of crime in Whitechapel.

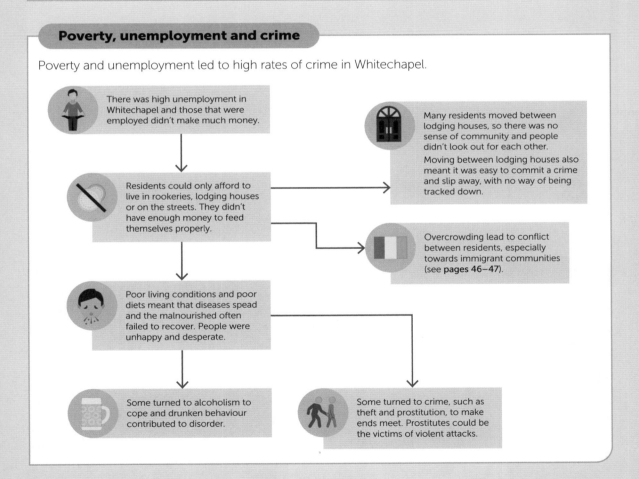

There was high unemployment in Whitechapel and those that were employed didn't make much money.

Residents could only afford to live in rookeries, lodging houses or on the streets. They didn't have enough money to feed themselves properly.

Many residents moved between lodging houses, so there was no sense of community and people didn't look out for each other.

Moving between lodging houses also meant it was easy to commit a crime and slip away, with no way of being tracked down.

Overcrowding lead to conflict between residents, especially towards immigrant communities (see **pages 46–47**).

Poor living conditions and poor diets meant that diseases spead and the malnourished often failed to recover. People were unhappy and desperate.

Some turned to alcoholism to cope and drunken behaviour contributed to disorder.

Some turned to crime, such as theft and prostitution, to make ends meet. Prostitutes could be the victims of violent attacks.

TENSIONS ARISING FROM THE SETTLEMENT OF IMMIGRANTS

Life was tough for everyone in Whitechapel, but the London-born residents often blamed immigrants for the poor living conditions.

Tensions arising from the settlement of immigrants

During the late 19ᵗʰ century, there was increased immigration in London. Devastating famines in Ireland had caused lots of Irish people to come to London in search of work and a better standard of living. Jews in Eastern Europe faced persecution, so many came to London hoping to escape discrimination.

Most immigrants arrived in London with little money, so they were forced to live in areas like Whitechapel. However, increasing immigrant populations led to tensions in the district.

 The surge in population in Whitechapel increased the competition for jobs. Some immigrants were prepared to work in **sweatshops** for low wages and in terrible conditions.

This angered Londoners who felt they were being squeezed out of the job market.

 The influx of immigrants worsened the issue of over-crowding in Whitechapel.

 Immigrants lived close together, which created segregated communities.

 Jewish people had their own language and culture which made Londoners wary of them.

 Fenians were an Irish independence group. They had been responsible for bomb attacks in London, which made some Londoners distrustful of Irish people.

The growth of socialism and anarchism in Whitechapel

The 19th century saw a growth in two movements: **anarchism** and **socialism**.

Anarchists support the abolition of governments and positions of authority.

Socialists believe that everyone is equal and that wealth should be shared equally.

These movements were gaining momentum overseas, for example in Russia, and some immigrants who moved to London's East End brought news of these movements with them. For the poverty-stricken people of Whitechapel, the abolition of the government and the fairer distribution of wealth seemed attractive.

The government, along with people with money or who had positions of power, wanted to stop anarchism and socialism from spreading.

An engraving of a socialist rally in London, 1892. A police officer can be seen in the foreground.

Describe **two** features of immigrant communities in Whitechapel between 1870–1900. [4]

There was an increase in immigrants living in Whitechapel during the 19th century, particularly Jewish and Irish immigrants.[1] Immigrants chose Whitechapel because accommodation was inexpensive, and many immigrants didn't have much money.[1]

The increase in immigrant communities led to tensions with London-born residents of Whitechapel.[1] Some immigrant communities segregated themselves from Londoners, which created a feeling of mistrust between the groups.[1]

THE ORGANISATION OF POLICING IN WHITECHAPEL

Policing Whitechapel was a tough and dangerous job.

The work of the H division

Whitechapel is on the outskirts of London city centre (i.e. Greater London), so responsibility for policing the district fell to the Metropolitan Police (see **page 52**). Greater London covers an enormous area, and each district was policed by a different division. Whitechapel was policed by the **H Division**.

'Beat' officers from H division would walk around Whitechapel, patrolling the area to keep an eye out for anything suspicious, to deter people from committing a crime and assist with minor disturbances, such as dealing with drunks, traffic and people fighting.

There were 15 detectives from CID who were assigned to H division, and they investigated crimes, such as the Jack the Ripper case (see **page 50**).

The difficulties of policing the slums of Whitechapel

 The slums, courts and alleys of Whitechapel were dark, cramped and narrow. Criminals could easily hide or evade capture.

 Most locals didn't respect the police, so they were often unwilling to help with the police's investigations, and some would even attack officers.

 There were socialist and anarchist (see **page 47**) demonstrations that could turn violent.

 Many residents of Whitechapel were heavy drinkers. This increased criminal behaviour.

 Gangs in Whitechapel were responsible for organised crime, such as employing bands of pickpockets, illegal gambling and fights.
They also ran protection rackets, where they would demand money from local businesses in return for not harming their staff and premises.

 Crimes against Jewish people were frequent due to increasing tensions towards immigrants (see **page 46**).

 There were about 1,200 prostitutes in Whitechapel. This led to an increase in violence towards women.

The Whitechapel Vigilance Committee

In 1888, residents in Whitechapel formed a volunteer group known as the **Whitechapel Vigilance Committee** to try to protect the community from Jack the Ripper. The committee felt that the local police weren't doing enough to catch the perpetrator.

The group was formed by a builder called George Lusk, and consisted of 15 local shopkeepers and property owners. They paid unemployed men to patrol Whitechapel every night. The Committee asked the government to offer a reward for information about Jack the Ripper, but the government refused (possibly because it would have led to people submitting false tips in hope of receiving money), instead the Committee put up their own reward to try to catch the killer.

An engraving from 1888 showing members of the Whitechapel Vigilance Committee observing a suspicious man.

Describe **two** features of the Whitechapel Vigilance Committee. [4]

The Whitechapel Vigilance Committee was formed in 1888[1] by George Lusk and 15 other local businessmen.[1]

The Whitechapel Vigilance Committee was formed in response to the murders committed by Jack the Ripper[1] and the group paid unemployed men to patrol the streets at night to protect the community from the killer.[1]

INVESTIGATIVE POLICING IN WHITECHAPEL

The murders committed by Jack the Ripper in 1888 terrified (and fascinated) Whitechapel residents, as well as the wider population of London.

Jack the Ripper

Between 31st August and 9th November 1888, five women were murdered and mutilated in Whitechapel. All five women were suspected of being prostitutes. The brutal nature of these crimes led the police and public to believe that the same killer was responsible. He became known as **Jack the Ripper**. To this day, his identity has never been discovered.

Developments in techniques of detective investigation

Inspector Abberline headed H division's (see **page 48**) investigation into Jack the Ripper. H Division used various methods to try to help them catch the killer.

Sketches

The police made sketches of crime scenes to try to record evidence and compare crime scenes. However, the sketches were not especially accurate.

Photographs

Cameras were a relatively new invention, but they were used in the Ripper case, and photographs were taken to record some, but not all, of the crime scenes. Photos were black and white, grainy, and not the same quality of photos today.

Autopsies

Autopsies were performed on the victims. The manner of the victim's mutilations suggested that the killer might have had some knowledge of anatomy, for example, he might have been a butcher or a surgeon.

Appeal for witnesses

The police distributed about 80,000 leaflets in and around Whitechapel to encourage witnesses to come forward if they had information.

Conducting interviews

The police interviewed people who lived near the murder scenes and known associates of the victims to try to piece together what happened.

Cooperation between police forces

The investigation was initially lead by H division, but **Scotland Yard** (the headquarters of the Metropolitan Police) sent additional men from the force to assist with the case. The Metropolitan Police and City of London Police both wanted to solve the Ripper case, but rivalry between the forces meant they struggled to cooperate. For example, some anti-Jewish graffiti was found near a piece of evidence in the Ripper case. The City of London Police wanted to photograph it, but Charles Warren (see **page 53**), Chief Commissioner for the Metropolitan Police washed it away, fearing violence towards Jews.

Problems caused by the media coverage of the 'Ripper' murders

The Ripper case caught the media's attention and it received lots of coverage in newspapers and magazines. This coverage made the police's job harder.

The media often reported information which was untrue or unproven. This spread misinformation, such as the belief that the killer wasn't English. This prompted violence towards immigrants.

More people became aware of the case, but this led to some accusing innocent people which wasted police time.

Articles blamed the police for not finding the killer. This increased public dissatisfaction towards officers, and put even more pressure on the police.

Letters were sent to newspapers supposedly from Jack the Ripper, but most were fake. Some were sent by reporters trying to whip up a story to sell more papers.

The front page of a newspaper showing a police officer finding the body of a Ripper victim.

As well as the media, groups like the Whitechapel Vigilance Committee (see **page 49**) also interfered with police investigations, making the police's job more difficult.

THE NATIONAL AND REGIONAL CONTEXT

The police in London weren't always respected by the people they were trying to protect.

The Metropolitan Police

The **Metropolitan Police Force** was founded in 1829, and was responsible for policing the Greater London area. The very centre of London was policed by a different organisation: the **City of London Police**.

There was a rivalry between the two groups. This sometimes hindered investigations, such as during the Jack the Ripper case. See **page 51**.

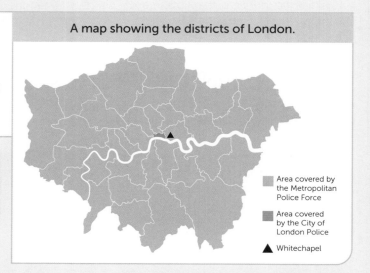

A map showing the districts of London.

Area covered by the Metropolitan Police Force

Area covered by the City of London Police

▲ Whitechapel

The role of the police

When the Metropolitan Police Force was first established, the quality of police recruits was generally poor. Being a police officer provided a steady wage, so people were attracted to the money, rather than a desire to become an officer, or because they were well-suited to the role. The training offered to new recruits was basic, and many officers didn't have the skills, equipment or the inclination to do their job properly.

The low standard of recruits meant that many people didn't respect the police.

Beat constables walked a set route in the district they patrolled to deter criminals and look out for anything suspicious. This was known as 'walking the beat'. Officers might be equipped with a lantern, whistle and a truncheon (a baton). These weren't adequate protection against criminals who were prepared to use knives or guns.

Some criminals knew the route taken by officers on the beat, so they committed crimes when they knew officers would be elsewhere on their route.

The development of the CID

By the 1870s, there was an expectation that police officers also needed to investigate and solve crimes, rather than just maintain a presence on the streets. In 1878, the **Criminal Investigation Department** (CID) was established. The techniques they developed were used in the Ripper case in 1888 (see **page 50**).

The role of the Home Secretary and Sir Charles Warren

The Metropolitan Police Force was under the control of the **Home Secretary** (a government minister), and the Home Secretary was responsible for appointing the **Commissioner of Police**, the most senior position in the Metropolitan Police Force.

Sir Charles Warren acted as Commissioner of Police between 1886–1888. A distinguished former soldier, Warren wanted to introduce more discipline into the police force. He clamped down on officers drinking on the job, encouraged ex-soldiers and farmers to join the force (Warren thought they would be stronger, more disciplined and less likely to be corruptible than men from the inner city). He expected recruits to be able to read and write, and he encouraged more military-style drills (i.e. marching practice).

Public attitudes towards the police

Some members of the public respected the police and saw them as necessary for controlling criminal activity in London.

However, the police were sometimes seen as:

Laughable

Charles Warren instructed officers to seize stray dogs. Many saw this as a waste of police time and believed the police should focus on more serious crimes, such as burglaries.

Unpopular

The police used unnecessary violence towards protesters in Trafalgar Square in 1887. This riot was known as **Bloody Sunday**.

Incompetent

Confidence in their abilities declined when they failed to catch Jack the Ripper in 1888 (see **page 50**).

The failings of the police force were often criticised or ridiculed in the press, which influenced public opinion. See **page 51** for more.

A new Home Secretary, Henry Matthews, was appointed in 1886, and he disagreed with Charles Warren both professionally and personally. Warren resigned as Police Commissioner in 1888.

A group of police officers walking the beat in London's East End at night.

Source A:

An extract from *Illustrated Police News*, a weekly newspaper, published on 8th September, 1888. The extract reports the police's efforts to find the killer of Mary Ann Nichols, the first known victim of Jack the Ripper.

Notwithstanding every effort the police engaged in investigating the murder of Mary Ann Nichols have to confess themselves baffled, their numerous inquiries having yielded no positive clue to the perpetrator of the crime. At the conclusion of the inquest Inspector Abberline and Inspector Helson were busily engaged in the matter, but have not elicited any new facts of importance. A large number of constables are engaged upon the case. Crowds of spectators continue to visit the scene of the murder in Buck's-row.

Source B:

A cartoon from *Punch* magazine from 22nd September 1888 entitled 'Blind-man's buff (As played by the Police). Turn around three times and catch whom you may'.

PUNCH, OR THE LONDON CHARIVARI.—September 22, 1888.

BLIND-MAN'S BUFF.
(As played by the Police.)
"TURN ROUND THREE TIMES,
AND CATCH WHOM YOU MAY!"

Make sure your answers are in paragraphs and full sentences. Bullet points have been used in the example answer to Question 1 to suggest some information you could include.

---

1. How useful are Sources A and B for an enquiry into the public opinion towards the police during the Jack the Ripper case (1888)?
   Explain your answer using Sources A and B and your own knowledge of the historical context.   [8]

2. How could you follow up Source A to find out more about the public's opinion towards the police during the Ripper case?
   In your answer, you must give the question you would ask and the type of source you could use.   [4]

1. Your answer may include:

   Source A:
   - Source A is useful because it suggests that the public were interested in the police's handling of the Ripper case because it made the local news.
   - Source A implies that the police are inept because it says the police are 'baffled' and 'have not elicited any new facts of importance'. This may have influenced public opinion about the police as it suggests that they are not making any progress with solving the murder.
   - However, the newspaper does admit that the police have made 'every effort' and that 'a large number of constables are engaged upon the case' which suggests that the police are putting a lot of resources into solving the murder, which may have reassured the public.
   - Source A may have been more lenient towards the police because this is a report about the first victim. There were four more victims between September and November, so public opinion towards the police probably worsened as there were more victims and no progress.
   - The police may have been reluctant to discuss new leads with the press because they didn't want sensitive information being publicised and the public interfering with their investigation.
   - The article was likely written by one journalist, so it only shows their perspective on the case.

   Source B:
   - Source B suggests that the police were ridiculed by the public, as the cartoon shows a police officer blundering about Whitechapel, being taunted by local residents.
   - The blindfolded policeman suggests that the public thought the police were 'in the dark' about the case, and had no leads to solve the Ripper case.
   - Publishing cartoons like this may have influenced public opinion by suggesting that the police were hopeless.
   - Punch was a satirical magazine, and would exaggerate topical issues for comic effect. Although there was some dissatisfaction towards the police, it may not have been felt by everyone or to this degree.

   Own knowledge:
   - Residents of Whitechapel (and London in general) disliked the police prior to the Jack the Ripper case, in part due to their handling of the demonstration in Trafalgar Square in 1887, so the public may have been overly critical of the police.
   - Some members of the public were so frustrated by the police's lack of progress they set up the Whitechapel Vigilance Committee to try to protect the local community and catch the killer.
   - The media made the police's job more difficult. For example, the criticism of their handling of the Ripper case eventually led to the resignation of the Police Commissioner, Charles Warren in 1888, so a new Police Commissioner had to be appointed mid-way through the case.

2. **Detail in Source A that I would follow up:** 'Inspector Abberline and Inspector Helson … have not elicited any new facts of importance'[1]

   Question I would ask: Did the police report anything to the press to reassure the public that they were conducting a thorough investigation?[1]

   What type of source I would look for: Interviews with or comments from the police in the local press.[1]

   How this might help me to answer my question: There may be quotes from these officers about the steps they were taking to try to catch the killer which may have reassured the public.[1]

   The answer to Question 1 should be marked in accordance with the levels-based mark scheme on page 67.

KNOWLEDGE OF NATIONAL AND LOCAL SOURCES

Questions 2(a) and 2(b) will be source questions. You need to know about the different types of national and local sources which might be used in enquiries.

Local sources

Housing, workhouse, council and employment records – Official records can provide useful statistics. They tend to be impersonal and factual.

Local police records – Police records can give first-hand information about crimes.

Coroners' reports — Provide information about the injuries sustained in a murder case.

Census returns – The **census** takes place every 10 years. It records who lives at a particular address, how old they are and what their jobs are.

Charles Booth's survey – Charles Booth was a businessman who was shocked by the conditions that poor people lived in. Between 1886–1903, Booth investigated poverty in London, and published his survey, *Life and Labour of the People of London*.

Photographs – Provide a real-life snapshot of Whitechapel and its residents.

London newspapers — Covered stories that local residents would find interesting.

National sources

Old Bailey records — The Old Bailey is the main criminal court in the UK. Every trial is documented, with details about the defendant, nature of the crime and the punishment received. These records tend to be factual and impersonal.

Records of crimes and police investigations — The police have kept criminal records since 1869. These records can give information about the types of crimes committed, and whether an individual is a repeat offender.

***Punch* cartoons —** *Punch* was a satirical weekly magazine established in 1841. It featured cartoons which often made fun of the government or famous individuals. Their articles and images can be useful to help understand the feeling of the general public, but they are often exaggerated.

National newspapers — If a story about Whitechapel featured in a national newspaper, this suggests that the story was important enough to have nationwide appeal.

STRENGTHS AND WEAKNESSES OF DIFFERENT SOURCES FOR SPECIFIC ENQUIRIES

For both source questions in the exam, you need to know about the strengths and weaknesses of different sources for a specific enquiry.

What is an historical enquiry?

An enquiry is the specific topic that a historian is researching. Examples for this course might be:

1. Enquiry into the types of crimes committed in Whitechapel in the period 1870–1900.
2. Enquiry into the impact of the Peabody Estate.
3. Enquiry into the failures of the police investigation into Jack the Ripper.

The usefulness of sources

A source cannot be judged on its usefulness without knowing the enquiry. For example, police records from 1888 would not be very useful for enquiry 2. However, it would be of some use for enquiry 1 and it would be useful for enquiry 3.

How to assess usefulness

There are three aspects to consider when assessing the usefulness of a source. You need to consider all three of these to achieve good marks for question 2(a):

The source's content

Does the source contain anything related to the enquiry? How useful is this?

Your own knowledge

Does the source support or contradict what you already know?

The source's provenance

Do the **origins**, **nature** and **purpose** of the source make it more or less useful?

An illustration showing an alley in Whitechapel.

 All sources in the exam will have a caption. This will provide information about the source's provenance, which will help you evaluate the source's usefulness.

Strengths and weakness of different sources

No source is completely reliable, so make sure to think about what it can tell you, but also what its limitations may be.

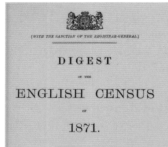

Census

- ⊕ Conducted by the government and contains fairly reliable data about the people of Whitechapel.
- ⊖ Only provides a snapshot of the population on one day in a ten-year period.
- ⊖ People who didn't have a fixed address might be left out of the census.

Photographs

- ⊕ Show what life was like in Whitechapel, and were more accurate than engravings or illustrations.
- ⊖ Might be posed or staged.
- ⊖ The photographer might work for a newspaper, and may have been told to take a photo which supports the angle of a news story, e.g. all residents of Whitechapel are lazy.
- ⊖ A photo only captures one moment, which might not be representative.
- ⊖ Usually in sepia or black and white, and the quality might be grainy.

Newspapers

- ⊕ Can reflect public opinion at the time, and the attitudes of journalists.
- ⊕ Report what was known about police investigations.
- ⊖ Stories were often sensationalised to increase sales.
- ⊖ Facts may be wrong or misreported.

These are just a few examples of some of the sources you might get in the exam. You might be asked to examine a source not covered on this page.

FRAMING QUESTIONS AND SELECTING SOURCES

In question 2(b), you will need to frame a suitable question and select appropriate sources to follow up a detail in the source provided.

Framing of questions

Any source will leave the reader with unanswered questions or information that they want to follow up.

- You must pick a detail from the source, either something you can see in an image or a written detail in a text source, and describe that detail.
- Use this detail to write a question to be investigated. It must relate to the detail, so if the detail is about policing, then the question needs to be directly relevant to this.

Selection of sources

Once you have decided on a question, you need to think of a source that would help you to answer this question. Your knowledge of the strengths and weaknesses of different sources will help with this (see **page 58**). For example:

- If your question is about housing, then a source related to accommodation would be helpful, such as council records or the census. Sources written by the government are more likely to be factual.
- If your question is about crime, then police accounts or records of trials from the Old Bailey could help with your enquiry.

Source C:

An engraving showing part of a street in Whitechapel in 1872. It featured in a book called *London: A Pilgrimage*.

Source D:
An extract from *Life and Labour of the People of London* by Charles Booth, published in 1889.

...much has been done for the clearing away of vile spots, which contained dwellings unfit for human use, and matched only by the people who inhabited them... the inhabitants of the slums have been scattered. Many people must have altogether left the district as the population showed a decrease of 5000 between 1871 and 1881; but with the completion of new buildings the numbers have again reached the level of 1871. Probably few of those who leave return; but it may be doubted whether those whose houses are pulled down are the ones to leave the neighbourhood... the vacant places are then taken by quite newcomers (in Whitechapel mostly poor foreigners) or by natural increase in the population.

Make sure your answers are in paragraphs and full sentences. Bullet points have been used in the example answer to Question 1 to suggest some information you could include.

1. How useful are Sources C and D for an enquiry into the problems facing residents in Whitechapel? Explain your answer using Sources C and D and your knowledge of the historical context. [8]

2. How could you follow up Source D to find out more about the problems facing residents in Whitechapel?

   In your answer, you must give the question you would ask and the type of source you could use. [4]

1. *Your answer may include:*

   Source C:

   - *The source shows lots of people in a small area, suggesting Whitechapel was overcrowded.*
   - *A group of children are sat in the street. Human waste often ran through the streets in Whitechapel, so this would have been unhygienic and may have contributed to disease.*
   - *Most people in the engraving seem to be loitering. This suggests that they don't have jobs to go to. Unemployment was a serious issue in Whitechapel.*
   - *The buildings appear to be in poor condition, suggesting they weren't properly maintained.*
   - *The people in the picture are wearing shabby and ill-fitting clothes, suggesting that they don't have the money to dress themselves properly.*
   - *The people seem unhappy, suggesting they are dissatisfied with life in Whitechapel.*
   - *Source C is an engraving, so it may not be entirely accurate. It only shows a small part of a street in Whitechapel, so it doesn't show how widespread these issues were.*
   - *The engraving was published in a book, which suggests the problems faced by the people in Whitechapel had national interest. However, it may have been exaggerated to make the problems in Whitechapel seem more desperate.*

   Source D:

   - *Source D suggests that steps were taken to improve housing in Whitechapel by clearing away slum housing. The author says that the houses were 'unfit for human use' which suggests that the poor quality of housing in Whitechapel was a real problem.*
   - *Source D suggests that the people who lived in the slums were 'vile'. This suggests that some people felt that the problems in Whitechapel were caused by the residents.*
   - *Source D says that 'poor foreigners' came to live in Whitechapel. This suggests that there was an immigrant population which may have contributed to poverty and overcrowding.*
   - *Charles Booth conducted an independent investigation into poverty throughout London, so he was able to make informed judgements about the poverty he witnessed in Whitechapel.*

   Own knowledge:

   - *Rookeries in Whitechapel were areas of slum housing which were overcrowded, and their residents lived in unpleasant conditions.*
   - *The Peabody Estate was built on an area of slum housing which was torn down as part of the Artisans' and Labourers' Dwellings Improvement Act in 1875. This housing was an improvement, but many still could not afford to live there which worsened overcrowding.*

     This answer should be marked in accordance with the levels-based mark scheme on page 67.

2. **Detail in Source D that I would follow up:** *Immigrants are described as 'poor foreigners'.* [1]

   Question I would ask: *Were the majority of immigrants in Whitechapel unemployed?* [1]

   What type of source could I use: *Census data.* [1]

   How this might help me to answer my question: *It would help me to understand how many immigrants in Whitechapel had a job.* [1]

EXAMINATION PRACTICE

1. Describe **two** features of the media's involvement in the Jack the Ripper case. [4]

2. (a) Study Source A and Source B. How useful are Sources A and B for an enquiry into the difficulties faced by police officers in Whitechapel?

    Explain your answer, using Sources A and B and your knowledge of the historical context. [8]

> **Source A:**
> An extract from the *Pall Mall Gazette* (a London newspaper) published 4th November 1889. In the article, Inspector Moore describes some of the difficulties of policing Whitechapel.
> *Inspector Moore led the journalist through the network of narrow passageways as dark and loathsome as the great network of sewers that stretches underneath them a few feet below... "Now, you know, I might put two regiments of police in this half-mile of district and half of them would be as completely out of sight and hearing of the others as though they were in separate cells of a prison. To give you an idea of it, my men formed a circle around the spot where one of the murders took place, guarding they thought, every entrance and approach, and within a few minutes they found fifty people inside the lines. They had come in through two passageways which my men could not find."*

> **Source B:**
> A cartoon from *Punch*, 1881 titled 'An Unequal Match'.
>
>

(b) Study Source B.

How could you follow up Source B to find out more about the difficulties faced by police officers in Whitechapel?

In your answer, you must give the question you would ask and the type of source you could use.

Complete the table below. [4]

Detail in Source A that I would follow up:	
Question I would ask:	
What type of source I could use:	
How this might help answer my question:	

EXAMINATION PRACTICE ANSWERS

Section B has been covered before Section A to provide a greater background to Key Topic 5 - the Historic Environment.

1. Your answer may include: [4]

    In the period c1500–c1700, the death penalty was widely used for hundreds of crimes, including minor offences, such as cutting down trees. The authorities believed that the death penalty was an effective deterrent and was an appropriate punishment for wrongdoers.

    In the period c1900–present, the number of crimes that were punished with the death penalty were far fewer, and it was reserved for only the most serious offences, such as murder. By the 1960s, the authorities recognised that the death penalty was not a fair or effective deterrent and they suspended capital punishment from 1965, until the death penalty was abolished in 1999.

2. Your answer may include: [12]

    During the medieval period, witchcraft was considered a criminal offence, however, cases of witchcraft were only tried in Church courts. Since Church courts very rarely punished crimes with the death penalty, most people accused of witchcraft weren't executed.

    However, this began to change in the 1500s following Henry VIII's break from the Roman Catholic Church. The monarch now had more control over the court system, and cases that had previously been tried in Church courts, such as witchcraft, could now be tried in secular courts. This meant that witchcraft could now be punished by death. During the 1500s, the Tudor monarchs introduced several acts against witchcraft, although they mainly focused on punishing malicious acts of witchcraft, and didn't consider helpful acts of witchcraft a crime.

    The start of the 1600s marked a turning point for the crime of witchcraft. King James I was particularly fearful of witches, and he published a book called *Daemonologie*, where he discussed the existence of evil spirits and how witches should be punished. King James believed that all incidences of witchcraft should be punished as he believed that the Devil gave witches their power, so all witches were inherently evil. Thanks to the introduction of the printing press and his status in society, King James' book was popular and contributed to growing paranoia about witches. This paranoia worsened during the English Civil War, as the country was thrown into turmoil, and the political and economic upheaval meant that some people began blaming others for the situation, and accusations of witchcraft began to increase. In Essex and East Anglia in 1645, Matthew Hopkins began charging local communities to hunt down witches, and he accused around 300 people of being a witch, and approximately 100 people were found guilty and hanged.

    Following the death of Matthew Hopkins in 1647 and the end of the Civil War in 1651, accusations of witchcraft began to decrease as the country entered a period of stability. By the early 1700s, a growing number of people no longer believed in witches, partly due to an increased interest in rational, scientific thought. Laws concerning witchcraft were changed in 1736 and stated that anyone claiming to be a witch was actually a fraud, because magical powers didn't exist. Anyone found guilty of practising witchcraft was punished with a fine or time in jail. These changes to the law meant that witchcraft was no longer seen as a serious offence that should receive the death penalty.

3. Your answer may include: [16 + 4]

    Although I agree that the main purpose of punishment in the period c1500–c1900 was deterrence, towards the later part of the period there was a shift towards using punishments as an opportunity for reform and rehabilitation, as the authorities realised that harsh punishments were not always an effective deterrent.

    Firstly, from the late 1600s, more crimes became capital offences, and this marked the beginning of the Bloody Code. Over the next 200 years, 222 crimes became capital offences, many of which were minor crimes, such as cutting down trees. The authorities hoped the severity of the punishment would deter people from committing these crimes. However, the Bloody Code did not prove to be an effective deterrent, as crime rates did not drop. This is partly because some people needed to commit crimes, such as poaching, to survive. Furthermore, some juries were unprepared to hand down the death penalty for minor offences, so they often found the accused not guilty. This encouraged more people to commit petty crimes, because they believed they would not be punished if they were caught. In the 1820s, Robert Peel effectively ended the Bloody Code by reducing the number of capital offences. This suggests that by the early 1800s, the authorities recognised that severe punishments were not an effective deterrent.

    Secondly, in the period c1500–c1700, punishments often took place in public, in order to deter others from committing crimes. Sometimes these punishments focused on public humiliation, such as putting vagabonds in the stocks, whilst capital punishments, for example, burning heretics, aimed to shock and deter the onlookers from committing a similar crime. However, by the 19th century, it became clear that public executions were not an effective deterrent, as large crowds would gather and watch the execution as a form of entertainment, often cheering the criminal as a hero. Consequently, executions began to take place in private, and the last public execution occurred in 1868. Again, this suggests that by the 1800s, the authorities began to recognise that public executions were not a deterrent.

Thirdly, towards the late 1700s, the prison system began to expand. Although prison sentences were more lenient than a death sentence, they still aimed to deter criminals because prisons were crowded, unsanitary and unpleasant. However, prison reformers such as Elizabeth Fry and John Howard, began to put pressure on the government to improve conditions in prisons, and to place a greater emphasis on rehabilitation by teaching convicts skills that they could use outside of the prison, and encouraging inmates to focus on religion to reform their character.

These prison reforms led to the development of the separate system and the building of Pentonville prison. Pentonville aimed to reform criminals by isolating them from each other and only allowing them to see and hear the prison chaplain. However, over the following decades, the authorities were frustrated that the separate system didn't appear to reduce crime rates, and some critics claimed that the conditions inside Pentonville weren't enough of a deterrent, so from 1865, the Prisons Act introduced the silent system where convicts were forced to endure hard labour in silence instead, in the hope of being a more effective deterrent.

In conclusion, the primary focus of punishment in this period was deterrence, although the authorities recognised that some individuals could not be deterred from committing crimes, irrespective of the punishment. For example, severe punishments such as public executions did not seem to deter people, and neither did less harsh sentences, such as isolation. Thanks to the work of individuals, there was a move towards reform and rehabilitation that gained momentum towards the end of the period.

4. Your answer may include: [16 + 4]

Forensic science has had an enormous impact on criminal investigations, especially where there are no eyewitnesses to a crime, as it can provide investigators with information which can help them to identify a suspect. However, I believe that other developments in technology and equipment, such as computers and personal radios, have had a greater impact on police work since 1829.

One of the most significant advances in forensic science was the introduction of fingerprint technology. Forensic investigators can dust for fingerprints, allowing them to place specific individuals at the scene of a crime. This technology has been used since 1901, and it has enabled the police to compile a database of criminals' fingerprints, which can be cross-referenced whenever suspicious prints are found. If there is an exact match between the suspect and the scene of the crime, this can prove that a suspect was involved, allowing investigators to bring charges against the individual.

More recent developments in forensic science include matching DNA evidence (found in hair and blood) from a crime scene to a suspected perpetrator. If there is an exact match between DNA left at the crime scene and a suspect, this provides irrefutable evidence that the suspect was involved. This can make it much easier to successfully convict criminals.

Although forensic science is a valuable tool for investigators, many criminals now wear gloves to avoid leaving fingerprints, and DNA evidence is only helpful if you have a suspect that you can match it to. Therefore, the police cannot solely rely on forensics to track down criminals. One valuable development to police work over the past 200 years has been the development of computers, specifically the Police National Computer, a database of police records and information. This database allows the police to share and search records much more easily than ever before and means that officers can follow up leads more efficiently.

Furthermore, developments in communication, such as the introduction of radios in police cars in the 1930s and personal radios in the 1960s, means that local police officers can communicate with each other much more easily. This is especially useful when chasing down suspects or attending crime scenes, as it allows separate teams of officers to coordinate and support each other, making the job safer and more efficient.

In conclusion, although forensic science has been a significant development in police work, it can only lead to successful convictions when there is a suspect who matches the DNA or fingerprints. Secondly, DNA evidence has only been used since the 1980s, so it has had a limited impact in the past 200 years. However, radios have assisted police officers for almost 100 years since their introduction in the 1930s, and more recently, the PNC has enabled police forces to share information instantly across the country, so I believe technology has had a more significant impact on police work than forensic science.

1.   Your answer may include: [4]
      The Jack the Ripper case attracted a lot of newspaper coverage because the public were fascinated by it. However, the media
      involvement hampered the investigation because newspaper stories could include information which was untrue or unproven
      which spread misinformation and led to worsening tensions between Whitechapel residents. Newspapers also criticised
      the police's investigation into the case, which put even more pressure on the police to solve the murders, and led to public
      dissatisfaction towards the police force.

2.   (a) **Source A**

           The following points could be made about the source's content: [8]

           - The alleys are described as 'dark' and 'narrow' which suggests that they were difficult to patrol.
           - Inspector Moore confirms that the network of streets meant that it was very difficult for the police to see and hear
             other officers which meant that they could not protect or support each other easily.
           - There were hidden passageways in Whitechapel which allowed criminals to move about undetected.
           - The source only focuses on the difficulties of the environment of Whitechapel, and doesn't include information
             about other difficulties officers may have faced, such as hostile civilians or lack of training.

           The following points could be made about the source's provenance:

           - It is a first-hand account of the difficulties police officers faced when policing Whitechapel.
           - However, the police were criticised for not catching Jack the Ripper, so they may have wanted to exaggerate how
             difficult Whitechapel was to police in order to defend their inability to solve the case.
           - The interview was published in a newspaper which may have wanted to sensationalise how bad the conditions
             were in Whitechapel.

           Knowledge of the historical context could be used to support and assess the usefulness of the sources:

           - Whitechapel had narrow, dark streets. Often there was little light at night, so officers carried lanterns.
           - Whitechapel's rookeries were overcrowded, which made it easier for criminals to evade capture.

           Source B

           The following points could be made about the source's content:

           - The criminal has a gun, knife and metal bar, whereas the police officer only has a baton to protect himself.
           - The criminal is attacking the officer, which suggests that police officers had to defend themselves from violent
             criminals who were prepared to kill to escape capture. This also suggests that criminals did not fear law
             enforcement or the repercussions of attacking a policeman.
           - The police officer is by himself, suggesting that some officers had to deal with criminals alone.
           - The title of the cartoon 'An unequal match' suggests that Punch felt that police officers weren't properly equipped
             to defend themselves from attackers.
           - The cartoon only focuses on the difficulties officers may face from armed civilians, and doesn't include any
             information about other difficulties, such as witnesses not cooperating with investigations or lack of training.

           The following points could be drawn from the source's provenance:

           - *Punch* is a satirical magazine, so it may have exaggerated the problem to make the cartoon more shocking for its
             readers. However, *Punch* usually pokes fun at people in power, so it is surprising that the cartoonist appears to be
             defending the police.

           Knowledge of the historical context could be used to support and assess the usefulness of the sources:

           - Police were only equipped with a lantern, a whistle and a baton, so they weren't able to defend themselves from
             knives and guns.
           - Many people in Whitechapel did not respect the police, and were prepared to attack officers.

      (b) Your answer may include: [4]

           Detail in Source B that I would follow up: Some officers were threatened with guns. In the cartoon, the criminal is
                                                          pointing a gun at the police officer.

           Question I would ask: How many officers were shot by criminals in Whitechapel between 1870–1900?

           What type of source I could use: Police employment records.

           How this might help answer my question: These documents would record any officers injured or killed by
                                                        gunshot wounds.

LEVELS-BASED MARK SCHEME FOR EXTENDED RESPONSE QUESTIONS

Questions 2(a), 3, 4 and 5 require extended writing and use mark bands. Each answer will be assessed against the mark bands, and a mark is awarded based on the mark band it fits into.

The descriptors have been written in simple language to give an indication of the expectations of each mark band. See the Pearson Edexcel website for the official mark schemes used.

Question 2 (a)

Level 3 (6–8 marks)	• The answer gives a judgement on usefulness *for the specific enquiry* with valid criteria and developed reasoning. • The answer assesses the impact of content and provenance on usefulness. • The sources are analysed to support the argument. • The answer demonstrates contextual knowledge to interpret sources and assess usefulness.
Level 2 (3–5 marks)	• The answer gives a judgement on usefulness *for the specific enquiry* with valid criteria. • The answer assesses content and provenance. • There is some analysis of sources through selecting material to support the argument. • The answer demonstrates contextual knowledge to support comments on content and/or provenance.
Level 1 (1–2 marks)	• The answer gives a simple judgement on usefulness. • The answer gives undeveloped reasoning on content and/or provenance. • There is simple understanding of the sources and content is repeated. • The answer demonstrates limited contextual knowledge.
0 marks	• No answer has been given or the answer given makes no relevant points.

Question 3

Level 3 (3–4 marks)	• The answer analyses features of the period(s) to explain a similarity/difference. • The answer includes specific supporting information which shows good knowledge and understanding of the period(s).
Level 2 (1–2 marks)	• The answer offers a simple or generalised comment about a similarity/difference. • The answer includes generalised information about the topic which shows limited knowledge and understanding of the period(s).
0 marks	• No answer has been given or the answer given makes no relevant points.

Question 4

Level 4 (10–12 marks)	• The answer gives an analytical explanation which is focused on the question. • The answer is well developed, coherent and logically structured. • The information given is accurate and relevant to the question. • The answer shows excellent knowledge and understanding of the topic. • The answer includes information that goes beyond the stimulus points in the question.
Level 3 (7–9 marks)	• The answer shows some analysis which is generally focused on the question. • The answer is mostly coherent and logically structured. • Most of the information given is accurate and relevant to the question. • The answer shows good knowledge and understanding of the topic.
Level 2 (4–6 marks)	• The answer shows limited analysis, and not all points are justified. • The answer shows some organisation, but the reasoning is not sustained. • Some accurate and relevant information is given. • The answer shows some knowledge and understanding of the topic.
Level 1 (1–3 marks)	• A simple or general answer is given. • The answer lacks development or organisation. • The answer shows limited knowledge and understanding of the topic.
0 marks	• No answer has been given or the answer given makes no relevant points.

Question 5 – SPaG (Spelling, Punctuation and Grammar)

High 4 marks	• The answer uses consistently accurate spelling and punctuation. • The answer uses grammar correctly and effectively. • The answer includes a wide range of specialist terms, where appropriate.
Intermediate 2–3 marks	• The answer largely uses consistently accurate spelling and punctuation. • The answer uses grammar correctly. • The answer includes a good range of specialist terms, where appropriate.
Threshold 1 mark	• The answer shows a reasonable level of correct spelling and punctuation. • The answer shows some control of grammar, and errors do not hinder meaning. • The answer includes a limited range of specialist terms, where appropriate.
0 marks	• No answer is given, or the answer does not relate to the question. • The answer does not meet the threshold performance level, and errors severely hinder meaning.

Question 5 – Content

Level 4 (13–16 marks)	• The answer gives an explanation with analysis which is consistently focused on the question.
	• The answer is well reasoned with supporting evidence, and it is clear and well organised.
	• The answer includes accurate and relevant information that has been appropriately selected to answer the question directly.
	• The answer shows broad knowledge and clear understanding of the topic.
	• The answer reaches a well-supported and clear judgement.
	• The answer includes information that goes beyond what has been mentioned in the stimulus points.
Level 3 (9–12 marks)	• The answer gives an explanation with some analysis which is largely focused on the question.
	• The answer is fairly well reasoned with supporting evidence, but it may lack some clarity and organisation.
	• The answer includes accurate and relevant information, with good knowledge and understanding of the topic.
	• The answer gives an overall judgement with some justification, but some supporting evidence is only implied or not correctly used.
Level 2 (5–8 marks)	• The answer shows limited or unsupported analysis of the question.
	• There is limited development and organisation, and the reasoning is not sustained.
	• The answer includes some accurate and relevant information, that shows some knowledge of the topic.
	• The answer gives an overall judgement, but it is not fully justified, or the justification is weak.
Level 1 (1–4 marks)	• A simple answer is given, which lacks development and organisation.
	• The answer shows limited knowledge and understanding of the topic.
	• The answer doesn't provide an overall judgement.
0 marks	• No answer has been given or the answer given makes no relevant points.

INDEX

ACKNOWLEDGEMENTS

The questions in the ClearRevise textbook are the sole responsibility of the authors and have neither been provided nor approved by the examination board.

Every effort has been made to trace and acknowledge ownership of copyright. The publishers will be happy to make any future amendments with copyright owners that it has not been possible to contact. The publisher would like to thank the following companies and individuals who granted permission for the use of their images and extracts in this textbook.

All graphics and images not mentioned below © Shutterstock

Image on p12 – St Mary's Church, Beverston © John Corry / Shutterstock

Image on p14 – Woodcut of a man giving alms to a beggar, 1569, public domain image

Image on p16 – The Bellman of London, 1616 © Walker Art Library / Alamy Stock Photo

Image on p19 – Guy Fawkes and the Gunpowder Plot © IanDagnall Computing / Alamy Stock Photo
Guy Fawkes caught in the act © Heritage Image Partnership Ltd / Alamy Stock Photo

Image on p20 – Matthew Hopkins © Charles Walker Collection / Alamy Stock Photo

Image on p25 – Tolpuddle Martyrs by Clifford Harper, © TUC Tolpuddle Martyrs Museum

Image on p26 – Muggers captured © Chronicle / Alamy Stock Photo

Image on p30 – Convicts exercising in the yard at Pentonville prison, 1862 © Chronicle / Alamy Stock Photo
Pentonville prison cell © Chronicle / Alamy Stock Photo

Image on p31 – A group of Robert Peel's first police officers © Trinity Mirror / Mirrorpix / Alamy Stock Photo

Image on p32 – The scene of the Omagh bombing © PA Images / Alamy Stock Photo

Image on p33 – Drug detection dog at the airport © Dragosh Co / Shutterstock

Image on p36 – Community Support Officers © Juiced Up Media / Shutterstock.com

Image on p41 – Dyce Conscientious Objectors, 1916 © Archive PL / Alamy Stock Photo
A British anti conscientious objector postcard published during WW1 © Pastpix / TopFoto

Image on p42 – Derek Bentley © PA Images / Alamy Stock Photo

Image on p44 – London lodging house, 1870 © Pictorial Press / Alamy Stock Photo

Image on p47 – Socialist meeting © Lanmas / Alamy Stock Photo

Image on p49 – Members of the Vigilance Committee scrutinise a suspicious looking man
© The Granger Collection / Alamy Stock Photo

Image on p51 – A policeman finding the body of Mary Ann Nichols
© Science History Images / Alamy Stock Photo

Image on p53 – Policemen on night patrol in the East End of London © Chronicle / Alamy Stock Photo

Text on p54 – Extract from the *Illustrated Police News*, 8th September 1888, reproduced from the British Newspaper Archive

Image on p54 – Jack the Ripper Punch Cartoon, 1888, Blind-Man's Buff
© Historical Images Archive / Alamy Stock Photo

Image on p57 – Alley in Whitechapel © Artokoloro / Alamy Stock Photo

Image on p58 – Census 1871, Wellcome Collection
– 'Hookey Alf' of Whitechapel, 1877 © Album / Alamy Stock Photo
– Front page of the *Illustrated London News* © f8 archive / Alamy Stock Photo

Image on p60 – Wentworth Street, Whitechapel, 1872 © The Print Collector / Alamy Stock Photo

Text on p60 – Extract from *Life and Labour of the People in London* by Charles Booth, Wellcome Collection

Text on p62 – Extract from the *Pall Mall Gazette,* 4th November 1889, reproduced from the British Newspaper Archive

Image on p62 – An Unequal Match © Punch Limited

EXAMINATION TIPS

With your examination practice, use a boundary approximation using the following table. Be aware that boundaries are usually a few percentage points either side of this.

Grade	9	8	7	6	5	4	3	2	1
Boundary	83%	74%	66%	58%	50%	42%	30%	19%	8%

1. Make sure your handwriting is legible. The examiner can't award you marks if they can't read what you've written.

2. Read the questions carefully. Don't give an answer to a question that you think is appearing (or wish was appearing!) rather than the actual question.

3. In Q2(b) you'll be asked about one of two sources. Make sure you write about the source specified in the question. If you write about the wrong source, you won't get any marks, no matter how good your answer is.

4. Don't spend too long on Q1, 2(b) and 3 as they're only worth 4 marks each. Make sure you've left yourself plenty of time to answer Q4 and 5/6 since they're worth 12 and 20 marks.

5. For the Thematic Study, make sure you know exactly which time period you are being asked about and if it has an alternative name (medieval period, early modern period etc). Remember that the 19th century refers to the 1800s, not the 1900s!

6. To get top marks in Q4 and 5/6, you need to include information beyond what is provided in the bullet points. Jotting down a quick plan before you start can help make sure your answer includes sufficient detail and is focused on the question.

7. Your answers to Q4 and 5/6 need to show breadth, i.e. include examples from across the time period you've been asked about.

8. In the longer written questions, use linking words and phrases to show you are developing your points or comparing information, for example, "as a consequence", "this shows that" and "on the other hand". This helps to give your answer structure, and makes it easier for the examiner to award you marks.

9. Your answer to Q5/6 will be marked for correct spelling, punctuation and grammar, as well as using topic-specific vocabulary correctly. Don't throw away marks by using casual language, poor spelling and no paragraphs.

10. If you need extra paper, make sure you clearly signal that your answer is continued elsewhere. Remember that longer answers don't necessarily score more highly than shorter, more concise answers.

Good luck!

These guides are everything you need to ace your exams and beam with pride. Each topic is laid out in a beautifully illustrated format that is clear, approachable and as concise and simple as possible.

They have been expertly compiled and edited by subject specialists, highly experienced examiners, industry professionals and a good dollop of scientific research into what makes revision most effective. Past examination questions are essential to good preparation, improving understanding and confidence.

- Hundreds of marks worth of examination style questions
- Answers provided for all questions within the books
- Illustrated topics to improve memory and recall
- Specification references for every topic
- Examination tips and techniques
- Free Python solutions pack (CS Only)

Absolute clarity is the aim.

Explore the series and add to your collection at **www.clearrevise.com**

Available from all good book shops

New titles coming soon!

PG ONLINE
2021 Winner 2022 Winner
Maths**Practice**
Step-by-step guidance and practice
Edexcel GCSE
Maths
Foundation 1MA1

PG ONLINE
2021 Winner 2022 Winner
Clear**Revise**
Illustrated revision and practice
OCR
Creative iMedia
Levels 1/2
J834 (R093, R094)

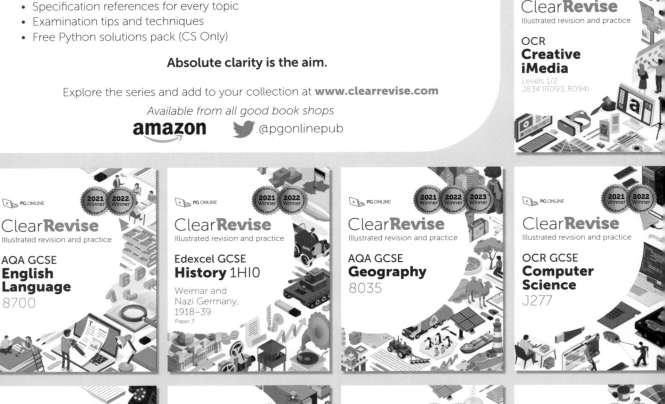